A Nice Boy from a Good Family

*Diaries, Essays, Memoirs, & Mostly True Stories
about Love, Lust, Life & Death*

First Edition

Published by The Nazca Plains Corporation
Las Vegas, Nevada
2009

ISBN: 978-1-935509-58-5

Published by

The Nazca Plains Corporation ®
4640 Paradise Rd, Suite 141
Las Vegas NV 89109-8000

© 2009 by The Nazca Plains Corporation. All rights reserved.
No part of this work may be reproduced or utilized in any form or by any means, electronic or mechanical, including photocopying, microfilm, and recording, or by any information storage and retrieval system, without permission in writing from the publisher. Printed in the United States of America.

PUBLISHER'S NOTE
This work is primarily one of nonfiction. Names, dates and places were changed to protect the anonymity of the living. Only a few friends and acquaintances with whom the author had only social contact (most notably Dossie Easton and Gayle Rubin) and the deceased are named with impunity.

Cover Model, David May
Cover Photo, Doug Campbell
Art Director, Blake Stephens

Dedication

Once again, for Phil, *aka* Sir, *aka* Sweet Daddy

―――――――

I never travel without my diary. One should always have something sensational to read in the train.
– Oscar Wilde

Acknowledgements

The Lousy, Rotten, No-Good, Son-of-a-Bitch, Goddamn Bastard first appeared in *Boy Friends from Hell*, Green Candy Press, 2003, edited by Kevin Bentley.

Something Sensational to Read in the Train first appeared in *Afterwords: Real Sex from gay Men's Diaries*, Alyson Books, 2001, edited by Kevin Bentley.

An Amsterdam Night first appeared in *Bar Stories*, Alyson Books, 2000, edited by Scott Brassart. It also appeared in *Unzipped* #182, 14 September 1999.

Mein Yiddisheh Tateh first appeared in *Kosher Meat*, Sherman Asher Publishing, 2000, edited by Lawrence Schimel.

"And what shall I do in Illyria?" first appeared in *San Francisco Frontiers*, Volume 13, Issue 24, 30 March 1995.

Life after Life first appeared in *San Francisco Frontiers*, Volume 14, Issue 21, 15 February 1996.

Hole first appeared in *Drummer* #197, July 1996.

Falling into the Cyber Dungeon first appeared in *San Francisco Frontiers*, Volume 15, Issue 2, 27 February 1997.

I Bought the Plot – *Now What?* first appeared in *San Francisco Frontiers*, Volume 16, Issue 2, 22 May 1997.

How I Fell in with the Wrong Crowd first appeared in *San Francisco Frontiers*, Volume 15, Issue 11, 26 September 1996; and in *Frontiers News Magazine*, Volume 15, Issue 11, 4 October 1996.

Looking for Venice first appeared in *San Francisco Frontiers*, Volume 15, Issue 14, 7 November 1996; and in *Frontiers News Magazine*, Volume 15, Issue 14, 15 November 1996.

Having Once Known Abandon first appeared in *Bad Boys: Steamy True Stories from Bathhouses, Backroom Bars and Sex Clubs*, Alyson Books, edited b Paul J. Willis and M. Christian.

Saying *Kaddish* first appeared in *Mentsch*, Alyson Books, 2004, edited by Angela Brown.

Damn the Defining first appeared in *San Francisco Frontiers*, Volume 20, Issue 11, 20 September 2001.

A Nice Boy from a Good Family

*Diaries, Essays, Memoirs, & Mostly True Stories
about Love, Lust, Life & Death*

First Edition

David May

Contents

The Seduction of an Innocent	1
The Lousy, Rotten, No-Good, Son-of-a-Bitch, Goddamn Bastard	7
Something Sensational to Read in the Train	15
An Apparent Proximity	53
An Amsterdam Night	65
Mein Yiddisheh Tate	71
Two Weddings, One *Tuchas*	77
"And what shall I do in Illyria?"	93
Life after Life	97
Hole	101
Falling into the Cyber Dungeon	111
I Bought the Plot – *Now What?*	117
How I Fell in with the Wrong Crowd	121

Looking for Venice	127
Having Once Known Abandon	133
Saying *Kadish*	145
Damn the Defining	151
An Afterward	157
About the Author	161

The Seduction of an Innocent

*There's a fine line, I think, between loving your
parents deeply and resenting them.*
– Roald Dahl

I can't remember exactly when it happened, but it was sometime after we moved from the suburbs of Washington, DC, where I had started reading comic books, to the suburbs of Long Beach, California, when my already voracious reading became my primary refuge. I was eight years old, the youngest of four, and often felt overshadowed by the brilliance of my elder siblings. In the world of my imagination, however, the one populated by characters from world mythology and the DC Comic Book Universe, I was the central player.

Until my discovery of superhero comic books, the object of my obscure desire was Guy Williams as Zorro. He had been my hero since age four; I even had a Zorro costume from Sears that I was allowed to wear at times other than Halloween. I imagined myself clinging to his adult frame on the back of his black stallion, and spent uncounted hours watching him on TV, reading not very good comic book adaptations of the TV series, and dreamily gazing at a pin-up on the back of one of the comic books. I didn't understand what I was feeling, but I knew enough to keep it a secret.

At about the same time I started reading superhero comics (as opposed to my sister's Archie Comics, or the Gold Key Comics – including Zorro, that my mother bought for us, or the Harvey Comics I had cut my teeth on as a beginning reader), I also came to the conclusion that adults were the enemy. They were an arbitrary authority, holding all the power, and to my mind consistently unreasonable. Rebellion seemed a sensible response, but being who I was, well brought up to a fault (dazzling my friends' parents with my good manners and polite interest in their tropical fish tanks and clock collections), my rebellion had to be covert. My goal was the undermining of adult authority through subtle, manipulative maneuvers. Overt action, open and angry revolt (for that was my dream), I saved for the imaginary world I inhabited when alone, one formed primarily from the old DC Comics Multiverse, and consisting of enough multiple Earths and alternative universes to do Schrödinger proud.

In that world I was a super-powered entity, independent of adult authority or power – no Robin to any Batman. I was neither wholly good nor evil, so much as a disrupter of adult complacence. In my pretend world I formed an alliance with Catwoman (an early role model even before the **Batman** TV show, important because she acted outside the law and yet was not essentially evil), Catman (less of a role model than a fashion statement since he was consistently less successful than the female original), the Trickster, the Teen Titans, Jimmy Olsen, Super Girl, the Cheetah, the Legion of Super Heroes, and always with the same goal of frustrating adult authority and winning those silly juvenile sidekicks over to my cause. In short, I sought the experience that Dr. Wertham had warned our parents about in his *Seduction of the Innocent* but, not finding it, I created it for myself.

One of my favorite stories of that time was **The Midnight Raid of the Robin Gang** (*Detective* #342). It was everything I hoped for, even when it failed to deliver: Robin stayed good all the way through the story, only pretending to be bad as he went undercover. I knew, though, that if I had my way with him (so to speak), he'd come around to my side. My fascination with his conversion to my cause bordered on the erotic.

Not long after, in *The Brave and the Bold* #54, the Teen Titans appeared for the first time. Cool, I thought, just what I need to mess with the Justice League of America and the rest: A group of goodie-goodies who will soon fall into my power, and then.... What? I can't remember all the plots I instigated, or how many succeeded or failed. I went to bed each night to think my nefarious plans through, letting them play out under the control of my subconscious (or so I now assume.) I must have lost more often than I won, and my few victories must have been far from complete, or I shouldn't have been able to continue with the storyline indefinitely. If I won, there could be no story: how would I then vent the powerless rage that often consumed me?

Occasionally friends joined me in acting out some of my fantasies, though they never seemed to grasp my focus in the game. This is how I learned that my plot to remove adults from authority was a lost cause: There were very few kids willing to go along with me. They *wanted* to be Robin, Wonder Girl, Speedy, Kid Flash or Aqualad. If nothing else, I'm sure they all believed that they'd always win in the end if they sided with the good guys. Well, if they did always win, I at least had the satisfaction of retaining my childish integrity. But never mind them: My pretend world was already populated with other like-minded, like-powered youngsters on my side. A few were based on my friends' fantasy personas, others were pulled from my imagination and often based on the crushes I had on older boys. Together, I imagined, we were a powerful force, and certainly more powerful than any dimwitted Crime Syndicate of America on Earth Three – adults hardly worth attending to – and capable of changing the adult-dominated world.

I remember very clearly sitting in our living room rather late one hot, humid summer night, reading an early issue of *The Teen Titans*. I don't recall where the idea first came from, but I decided that what I needed to do was convince Robin and the gang to attend a party I'd give in their honor. I was rather vague on the exact content of this Bacchanalia (for I was only ten) and even less clear was the precise nature of the debauchery I already craved. My vision of the party's conclusion, however, included the various Teen Titans passed out and sprawling around my parents' living room (now transported to a penthouse apartment in either Metropolis or Gotham City) as I sat by, satisfied with the damage done and the results of my Nefarious Plan. When the Teen Titans awoke from what I can only now guess was some sort of magical drugged stupor, they would be "mine at last." The plot must have failed in the end, though I'm sure that I managed to escape back to my home planet (for I could not be my parents' child and still be super-powered) to hatch yet another scheme.

My home planet, naturally enough for a boy whose first word was "kitty," was a world ruled by cats. Not only would adult authority be subverted, you see, but human authority. I imagined in lurid detail a feline take over of the planet. Cat lovers would hold exalted positions; those who hated or harmed cats were executed in appropriately grisly fashions, while the rest of the non-cat worshipping population was allowed to live on as servants to the feline elite – of which I was a leading member, of course. This epic fantasy led to my continued alliance with Catwoman, the only adult to whom I might have consented to be a kid sidekick, but even then my extraterrestrial feline origin made me much more than a mere protégé. Like the blessed Selina Kyle herself, I was independent and autonomous, my only emotional attachment belonging to my feline companions.

Things, of course, changed with adolescence. I still loved cats, but the nature of the love I felt for male comic book characters altered, then evolved. More significantly, the very object of my love, once mutable and vague, polymorphous as perversity itself, solidified into the archetype against which all men would someday be measured. However much my relationship with Robin bordered on the seductive, however jealous I might have been of the Teen Titans, or even Batman, my childish crushes on Batman and Robin never saw fruition, let alone consummation. Now, like a baby bird that imprints on the first thing it sees, so I imprinted on the single sexual object that presented himself to me from the pages of my comic books when puberty struck. With him I first faced the core of my desires.

I discovered him at the same moment I discovered how good it felt to stroke my dick, and many of my earliest sexual fantasies revolved around him – Marvel Comics' Nick Fury. He was big, burly, mean, hairy, unshaven, cigar smoking, insensitive and violent: In short, he was my kind of man: Nick *Fucking* Fury! He was my secret, like my best friend's *Playboys*, wrinkled and cum stained and hidden beneath the mattress, only I was allowed to read *Nick Fury Agent of S.H.I.E.L.D.* openly. I remember jerking off while looking at images of Nick Fury sprawled in a chair with only a towel to cover his nakedness, or nearly nude in bed amidst a sea of disheveled sheets, sheets rumpled in a way I would only later recognize as post-coital.

I imagined myself in his world, being his fellow agent and, more importantly, his catamite. I thought of myself in his bed, warm and safe, at the end of our adventures, being held against his hairy chest, feeling his stubble against my face, smelling his cigars on my clothes. My idea of what we did in bed was vague at best, unformed fantasy. I knew only that I wanted to belong to him, merge with him, and smell him on person. No other comic book character could ever have this effect on me, not even Zorro.

During those same hormone fraught age when absolutely everything is infused with erotic possibilities (however unclear and unformed they be in one's ignorant imagination), I stumbled across, purely by accident, lying along the side of the road, a copy of DSI Publication's *Butch* #10. I was shocked and thrilled that such a thing existed (as I'd been certain it must) and shoved the small magazine in my pocket, got back on my bike with the butterfly handlebars, and continued with my normal Saturday of racing around to make my weekly comic book purchases. Now and then, when I was sure no one could see me, I pulled the little magazine out of my pocket to verify that I did indeed possess what I thought I'd found: Pictures of naked men. Once home, I ran immediately to my room to hide my contraband. Eventually I decided on the bottom of my junk drawer amidst scrapbooks, marbles, magic markers, and other treasures. Inserting it in an envelope shuffled amidst other envelopes containing my first theatre program (**You're a Good Man Charlie Brown** starring Gary Burghoff), travel brochures for places I longed to visit, magazine articles, *National Geographic* maps, puzzle books, and old catalogues, I was unlikely to be found out. Our family's respect for privacy was my best protection against discovery. Discretion and a closed door were all I required to enjoy my new discovery.

Now that I knew this other world existed, I actively pursued it: I looked for traces of Nick Fury in my friends' Dads, in my gym teachers, in the biker movies I soon became addicted to, in my Dad's fellow Naval officers, in the enlisted military men I saw on the streets of San Diego (where we moved when I was thirteen), in the men sun bathing at the beach, in any man on a motorcycle. I longed for their touch, to be their victim, to be the one they hurt and held in affection, to be kissed and abused, to know pleasure and pain, to be always afraid and excited when they looked my way. As a young man I searched for him among my teachers, among the upper-classmen at the gym, and finally on the streets of San Francisco.

My interest in comic books came and went over the years, but not my fixation on Nick Fury, or the standard he set when my deepest desires came to fruition. I found Nick Fury's clones in the Fire Island meat rack and the bars along San Francisco's Folsom Street, men promising to love me enough to hurt me. Eventually *Drummer* magazine canonized his image in the icon of the Leather Daddy, and John Preston dubbed him Mister Benson in his serialized novel of the same name. It was in their arms, and by their hands, that I finally found myself, where I first felt the terrible touch that would rival all my fantasies, and in their embrace I first met that authentic authority to which I would gladly submit.

The Lousy, Rotten, No Good, Son-of-a-Bitch, Goddamned Bastard

Virginity of its very nature makes danger from within for its possessor.
– Kate O'Brien

Whenever the topic of First Love comes up in conversation, I always say (*a la* Kay Medford in **Funny Girl**): "That lousy-son-of-a bitch-goddamned-bastard? Where ever he is, he should only stay there!" Which always gets a laugh and excuses me from elaborating on a story more embarrassing than provocative. How I envy those who had sex with other boys in high school, the ones who fell in love with their college roommates, the ones who just played the field during those brilliant first few years of young manhood. Young love, I now know, is a precious thing, and it's a disservice to the young not to tell them this, not to let them know that this is the love they will remember their whole lives, whatever the outcome. As I write this, I don't know whether my first love, Doug, is alive or dead. I no longer know anyone who might be able to tell me. But best, or perhaps saddest, of all, I don't give a good goddamn.

I was almost nineteen when I met Doug. It was 1974 and sex between men was still a crime in the State of California (and would be for a few more months), though convictions were hard to come by unless the charge also included public lewdness. Doug was a product of those years when gay men were routinely harassed, when arrests ended careers and lives. He was what I later knew, pejoratively, as a Fifties Queen: A product of the pre-Stonewall years, filled with self-loathing and afraid of his own queer shadow. How old was Doug when we met? I'll never know for certain. Over forty, certainly, because he admitted to being that old; but his age kept fluctuating between forty-three and fifty during the four years I knew him. Not that his age bothered me. He was handsome and initially very attentive to me; while I was shy, inexperienced, and more than a little *naïve*.

I met Doug through the parents of friends during my first year of college. Somehow or other I was invited to his home with a large group of people. He knew at once that I was gay – even though I was dating a girl, wondering if I was in love with her, and still unclear on the exact nature of my masturbatory fantasies wherein men were clearly pictured and women only vague shadows. On our second meeting he invited me to visit him for a weekend at his home in the Santa Cruz Mountains.

Seduction began, as it often did in those days, with an exchange of massages. Of course one muscle group led to another, and soon we were naked and he was fondling my dick. I got hard in seconds. He patted the spot on the bed next to him, and I wordlessly obeyed.

Then came my first real kiss. I'm sorry to say, I didn't much enjoy it. There may have been a myriad of other things wrong with that kiss, but the main trouble with it was that he smoked mentholated cigarettes and his mouth tasted icky. Kissing would eventually become my favorite activity, the one thing that would tell me everything I needed to know about a potential lover; but that first time with Doug, kissing was just nasty.

The sex was (as it so often is for virgins) disappointing. This probably had as much to do with me as with Doug. People raised Baptist or Catholic often say that the repressive nature of their religious upbringings got in the way of their enjoying life. For my part, while I was raised Unitarian, I also came from a long line of New England Puritans. My attitude towards my body, sexuality, and even bodily functions, was at best circumspect. I even masturbated by rubbing my dick against the mattress rather than using my hand and wouldn't master jerking-off manually for a few more years. So Doug's ministrations, his cock sucking, his caresses, were paid to a body that hardly knew how to respond to them. I eventually fucked him that night, cumming quickly (though not as quickly as he did when he fucked me a few minutes later), but didn't feel satisfied.

Doug must have sensed this and gave me a slow, methodical hand-job. At first I protested, saying that I wouldn't be able to cum again (as if I had any experience to judge from) to which he replied, "Let me surprise you." When I climaxed for the second time that night, I shot high into the air (I'm not exaggerating) and all over us. This cum shot to end all cum shots left me speechless and breathless, grateful for what he'd done for me, not knowing that this would be the first and last time he would ever be sexually generous towards me. I thanked him and he said the words I later came to hate him for:

"I love you."

Damn him to hell.

I didn't even know then, because no one had ever presented the possibility to me, that two men could love each other. They could fuck, of course – but love? And even though I'd had crushes on innumerable teachers, coaches and classmates before then, it had never occurred to me that I had been (however childishly) in love with them. Not knowing what else to do, I said, "I love you, too."

His lies began at once, the most prominent of which was that James Dean had been his lover. The story he told was convincing, and I, as hungry for glamour as the next baby *feygellah*, ate it up, eager to believe every word. To this was added the story that the famous former madam (and mayor of Sausalito) Sally Stanford had been a family friend, that he had appeared on Broadway in the original production of **Little Mary Sunshine** (the recoding of which was, he insisted, exceedingly rare and *not* the one I'd found in the library that had not included him), that he had fought in Korea where he held his dying lover in his arms, that he was a registered nurse with a doctorate in hospital administration, and that he knew Rock Hudson. Of all his tall tales, only the last one *may* have been true.

Before I went home two days later (days spent feeling like a heroine from a Colette novel and wanting to scream to the world, "I have a lover!") Doug gave me what can only be described as a man's cocktail ring. I've never been fond of (unattached) jewelry, and flashy jewelry on men is an instant turn-off for me. This ring was platinum with a yin-yang circle containing, in his words, "two small diamonds and a good ruby." It was too big for me and had to be worn on my pointer finger with a ring guard – and was about as vulgar as any piece of jewelry one might see outside of a Neiman-Marcus catalogue. I hated and loved it at the same time: And now I really was like a character from Colette, a courtesan infused with the glamour of being loved and given jewels.

Back on campus I looked up articles on James Dean at the university library (serious biographies of him were only just then being published, none of them yet available at the library) only to find holes in Doug's stories, incorrect dates, and impossible details. I didn't do the research to find fault with him, just to feel closer to him. When I later asked him about the inconsistencies he passed them off as the difference between the official story of Dean's life and the actual one. That he got the date of Dean's death wrong by ten years, though, I found profoundly puzzling and, of all the details to his tale, that one inaccuracy told me clearly (though I didn't wish to know it, lying being the one sin I can never forgive in a loved one) that Doug's whole life story was a fabrication.

He called me the day after our weekend together. He was clearly happy and infatuated with me, and I enjoyed being the object of his affection. Then his letters came, profuse and full of declarations of love, promises of where he would take me, and the wonderful things we would do together. Not knowing any better, I believed him; and believing him I responded with my own declarations of love in letters full of arms, legs, and lips.

Then, a few weeks later, the oddest thing happened: I *did* fall in love with him, and writing him one more time with that declaration I said, "Don't ever not love me!" Which was when, of course, he stopped writing, stopped calling, and stopped caring. The only thing that he continued to do was lie. And fuck me. But mostly he just lied.

At parties he would make claims that no one could easily refute: He created the logo for Hang Ten T-shirts; he managed a local jazz band; his doctor ordered him to drink *at least* three cocktails a day; he was intimate friends with this or that Broadway composer; he was the scion of an important California family; smoking was actually good for him. Whenever anyone might offer a story of his own to this party chatter, Doug would cut him off to regale us with yet another tale. Of all of these stories I was most amused at his bragging about his California antecedents. Being the offspring of New Englanders I lived with the contradictory teachings that one can neither take blame nor credit for one's ancestors; and, conversely, that our ancestry was something we were deeply proud of, if not a reason to feel superior. Doug bragging about his family was vulgar; his bragging about a mere four generations ludicrous. I repressed the contempt this aroused in me, suppressed it in lieu of sex, sex that was getting better and better with practice.

Now that I had told him I loved him, all his promises were broken. When I saw him he was brusque, even abrasive, until we were alone together and could fuck. During those moments he was his old sweet self, kind - almost loving. When it was over, after he came, I was pushed quickly away, out of his bed and out of his life. Being young and inexperienced, I lived for those furtive moments of joy in his arms. It didn't occur to me to look for affection (and sex) elsewhere – at least not at first. It wasn't until he announced that he "wasn't going to be gay anymore" and convinced a rather beautiful woman to marry him, that I allowed myself the luxury of tricking with my peers. He announced his engagement with no warning at a barbecue hosted again by my friend's parents and I, like another character from Colette (the mistress wronged) stormed out as quickly as I could without so much as a word – but with a lot of noise: doors banging, feet stomping, tires screeching.

Later he would say that he'd told me ahead of time: Another lie. As always, he thought that if he insisted a lie were true it would either become true, or he could at least convince others that it was true. That was our official break-up, and the first time I called him a liar, spitting the word as if it were a curse. He asked for his ring back and I threw it in his face in a dramatic gesture. I always regret succumbing to the theatrical at that moment. I wish to this day that I'd kept it as a trophy so I could at least say that I'd left the victor. If nothing else, in hard times I might have sold it.

I was furious and refused to see him anymore. Except that he kept coming around "to talk" and eventually convinced me to have sex with him. It was furtive sex, though, and left me feeling dirty (in a bad way, that is) and wanting nothing more to do with him. I contemplated exposing him with some dramatic gesture, but that was unnecessary. He fell in love with someone new, a married man this time, and cut his poor fiancée off without a word. While I occasionally saw the married man at the Dragon Moon (our local gay disco), he was clearly attached to his wife and children. Doug, unable to lure him away from his married life, became less and less discrete, eventually creating a scandal I heard whispered about for months to come. I said nothing when I heard it, only smirked to myself, content to be standing on the sidelines watching.

Having screwed with one person too many in a small town, and no longer able to live there comfortably, Doug needed to mask his departure in yet another cloud of deceptions. Now he was sick; now he had Huntington's chorea and was doomed to a slow miserable death; now he had had a heart attack; now we all had to feel sorry for him. He told everyone these lies, his friends and family, including his parents. He ran off to Carmel and another poor sap that was initially seduced by his charm but who, being worldlier than me, tossed him out when Doug began tripping over his lies.

It was around this time that I developed an addiction to Billie Holiday, especially the heroin and alcohol infused recordings that held enough vocal misery to ease the heartache I languished in as only the very young may. This was a behavior I would indulge in for years to come whenever a love affair ended, imagining it very sophisticated to sit in a dark room with a cigar and a Campari, weeping silently as Lady Day sang about the dark side of love.

My decision to fuck around was motivated by something I'd read in one of Colette's memoirs. Writing about her marriage to Willy - the man who took credit for her writing for so many years - a marriage that lasted most of her youth, she expressed regret that she had never known the joy of making love, while she was young, with a lover as young and supple as herself. In this regard at least, I did not want to be like her. So I went out looking for sex among my peers.

I've forgotten the boy's name, but we met at The Dragon Moon, and I brought him home. I remember that I enjoyed kissing him, that he had a beautiful butt, that we took turns fucking each other, and that for the first time I really enjoyed having a cock up my ass. I also remember not really liking him by the time we said goodnight and he went home. I don't recall speaking to him again, though I did see him around. He was my first real trick and an important rite of passage, both in getting over Doug and in becoming the kind of liberated gay man I wanted to be. I wasn't going to be afraid of discovery like Doug had been his whole life, nor would I accept dishonesty and self-hate as a way of life. I was part of that second wave of post-Stonewall gay men that (for better or worse) helped to define the 1970s, a decade that now seems strangely innocent: One where love knew no consequence beyond a broken heart.

The last time I saw Doug I was in Carmel while I was visiting the man Doug had run there to be with when he'd left Santa Cruz. Not unnaturally, we had come to be friends and fuck buddies, often sharing stories about Doug's pathological dishonesty. Conversation over brunch with friends that morning was, of course, primarily gossip, and Doug's name came up: Did we know that he had broken-up with his latest lover after only a few weeks? Did we know that this lover (a man I tricked with a month later as much out of spite as out of lust) had, while moving Doug's stuff out, found a letter from Doug's parents asking why Doug had lied to them about his supposed illness? Did we know he was working at an antique store for an even nastier, older queen than himself?

Then we moved on to his more outlandish lies: He was writing his memoirs (or a novel, depending to whom one talked) for which he claimed to have gotten a huge advance; he had been offered the management of an important hotel in Carmel but had turned down the job for reasons that were never explained; he was intimate friends with Bette Midler (whom he called Betty) and was writing the script for her first Hollywood movie. He had long since found a new group of friends he could waylay with his lies, dropping out of all of our lives. Carmel being a very small town, though, word of his whereabouts, schemes, lies and failures still reached us through the grapevine.

"Isn't he dead yet?" someone asked.

I joined in the roar of laughter realizing that no part of me loved him anymore. I'd had sex with him "one last time" a couple years before, partly out of pity and partly out of nostalgia: After that I had stopped caring altogether.

"You know, Dave," Doug had said as I'd left that day, "whatever you may think of me, I'm here for you."

I only nodded, knowing that the man was no more capable of telling the truth, or of loving someone, than he was of flying to the moon. Now, at brunch, I laughed at his expense, feeling no shame, and took delight in the further divulgences about him being offered over mimosas.

"He never even went to college, you know. He was a kept boy down in LA. A friend of mine in Newport Beach told me that he –."

"His own mother wouldn't let him kiss her. She said, 'I don't know where your mouth has been.' Or that's what I heard from –."

"Such a snob! Even for a queen, I mean. And everyone knows he's from fucking Fresno! That's where the Greyhound stops to pee!'"

"And that letter from his parents his ex found! That made the rounds!"

"What do people ever see in that silly queen?"

What indeed? I asked myself. No answer came.

Later that afternoon, driving through Carmel in my little, beat-up Volkswagon, I stopped at a crosswalk. There he was, crossing the street in front of me. His eyes focused on my windshield, on me in the driver's seat, and just as I saw recognition light his face, just as he realized I was in the car, I put the sunblind down so I needn't see him, nod, nor even greet him.

He crossed the street and I drove on, never looking back.

A Nice Boy from a Good Family

Something Sensational to Read in the Train

Keep a diary and one day it will keep you.
– Mae West

17 October 1978 (Carmel, California[1])

Called Robby on Sunday and made a lunch date in the City[2] for yesterday. Fool that I am, I arrived on time at 11:30 AM. He was running late. He showered/shaved while I read. Then he walked in and lay down next to me where I was reading on his bed. He kissed me. At first it was pleasant. But later when he fucked me I became so anxious that I lost my erection. I never fully got it back either. He tried to jerk me off but couldn't even get me hard.

---

1 I was living in Carmel, California at the start of this diary. Carmel is on the south side of the Monterey Peninsula, next to Pebble Beach, an hour south of Santa Cruz where I had attended university, and two or more hours south of where my heart lay in San Francisco. I am still mystified as to why I moved to Carmel rather than San Francisco after graduating,. Officially I was waiting tables and saving money for graduate school, though this was a lie, made mostly to myself. I visited San Francisco frequently until I moved back there in 1980, usually staying with a college friend.

2 San Franciscans never call their city Frisco. They just call it The City, a more pretentious appellation being unavailable.

Then we began foreplay all over again. I became almost completely erect and fucked him. I faked the orgasm. I felt like shit.

13 February 1979

Nick from New Jersey; of Greek descent. Dark, heavy stubble, *very* hairy. Forty-three years old; looks more like thirty-five. Not at all condescending. Appreciated both my maturity and *naïveté*. Appreciated both and was threatened by neither. Beautiful man. Not very tall, but a very sexy body. A nice face, the lines are deep but few, not a mesh of fine ones. A very masculine face, sexy. We fucked.

His whole body is brown and hairy – all over. His cock (of average size) was a youthful pink. It was so beautiful I had to suck it. I loved sucking it. I drove him wild licking his balls, cock and crotch, rimming him. I took his whole cock into my mouth and swallowed every drop of cum. Wanted more of the same sweet juice. Then I fucked his hairy, round ass.

"Do you want to fuck me? Let's see if you fit. I'm tight as a…"

He kisses like no one I know. He came toward me with an open mouth, like he was going to eat me. His rough-bearded face scratched mine. He would hold me down and lick my neck, driving me up the wall. He would lick my navel and suck my cock alternately. (Later: "You didn't know about your belly-button, did you? Watch that navel!") Threw me all over the bed. We would crush each other in our arms and legs. All over each other, often making love in wrestling positions. The sex was better than anything I ever had with Robby. Rough but never violent. Gentle at times, abrasive at others. He called out my name and grabbed my arm as I brought him to climax with my tongue and mouth. "Take it! I'm cumming! Take me!" I filled my mouth with his cock and swallowed him, took him inside me. Sweet cum. Not enough of it, though. A small load. Sweet, sweet cum.

Then today he invited me to New York this summer – and Fire Island!!

25 June 1979

Yesterday was Gay Freedom Day in San Francisco, the first day of the same week. I was freed in a matter of speaking, reaching new depths of degradation, seeking out still (by me) untried paths to sleaze, loosing myself to moral decay, as I had never done before.

After the Parade, Cary[3] and I went to the Castro and had dinner at the Neon Chicken. I had two Dubonnets before dinner while we waited upstairs to be seated, and two glasses of wine with dinner. So I was pretty tipsy when Cary and I left the restaurant. We walked along Castro Street, which was packed with men. We somehow managed to get into DJ's and onto the dance floor. They were playing Donna Summer's **Hot Stuff** when we came in. (We had walked down 18th Street after leaving the Neon Chicken singing and dancing to **Bad Girls**.) When the song segued to **Bad Girls** a leather man started feeling my ass and groping me as we passed, his buddy humping me. I grabbed the crotch of the first man.

"You *are* a bad girl!"

Then I humped his buddy.

The dance floor was packed with bodies wiggling like living sardines in a can. I groped ass to my heart's delight, getting the same. Such a hussy! (Earlier at the Celebration I had seen two leather men. One of them – tall, young and quite good looking – being jerked-off through his jeans by the other – not so tall, young or good looking as the first – who stroked him with one hand and pinched his nipple with the other. I was turned-on by the exhibitionism of it, being a voyeur.)

A man of about thirty, maybe five-foot four, bearded and moderately good looking, started dancing in front of me. The floor was so packed that people had come between Cary and me, anyway, and I supposed that the man was dancing with someone behind me, though I couldn't be sure. I had noticed him cruising me earlier, but hadn't paid much attention to him since I was with Cary and wasn't going to follow through with anything. Then he reached out and felt my chest. I returned the favor by rubbing his torso. He pinched my nipples. I pinched his. I looked over at Cary, who was laughing, and decided to see this thing through. We as yet hadn't stopped dancing. We progressed to groping buttocks and crotches, and finally kisses. Then he grabbed my hand and, without saying word, led me to the men's room. (Cary asked for the poppers as I passed him on the dance floor and I gave them to him.) We went into the only stall, which had no door, where we kissed and fondled each other, still saying nothing. Then he started to jerk us both off. When he came I reached down with my mouth for his cum, which dribbled over onto my moustache and chin. After that he asked my name. I asked his: Serge. He was French. I told him my situation that I was spending the day with my friend Cary but that I'd like to go home with him another time. He said no, that he

---

3 Cary Bobier, one of my best friends at the time, and a close friend until his death in 1993.

couldn't because he had an "old man" (whom I saw later, much older, probably a sugar daddy). We kissed and parted. I was amazed with myself. I couldn't believe that I just done what I had just done.

Later on we stopped at the Locker Room on Polk Street. I went back to the peep shows. There was a sign reading: Hustling and Soliciting Forbidden, but there were a lot of men cruising and a couple of what looked like hustlers. I went into a booth and saw, for a quarter, a bad JO film. Interesting but not exciting. That is, the experience, being new, was enjoyable, while the film was boring. Very sleazy. We went home after that. I am now ready for baths and backrooms. Am I jaded yet?

26 June 1979

I need to write more about Sunday. All of the Castro seemed to be in a sexual frenzy, like what I imagine the baths to be like. When we got onto the dance floor at DJ's I was immediately caught-up in the euphoria of it all. By the time the two leather men came around, I was totally without inhibitions and reacted to the groping in a way that I would have hitherto been embarrassed by: I *enjoyed* being what he called "a bad girl"!

Then there was Serge. I was also struck by that incident, by both his sexual aggressiveness and my own willingness to reciprocate. Simple, unadulterated lust. Very basic. And the coupling took place all around us, and seemed to happen very quickly, the usual hours of games cut to a few minutes on the dance floor with some necking, nipple pinching and groping. And then leaving with each other. One coupling struck me because it happened near where we were dancing. Both of them were blond, and about five-foot eight; the younger about twenty-two, the older about thirty. The older removed his shirt to the obvious delight of the younger. I watched, again the voyeur, as they stopped dancing, began kissing, licking and biting each other. A definite turn-on. And then they were gone, and all in about ten minutes. The sexual frenzy, I suppose. A great big, wonderful party. When we left I was so happy. I really didn't want to leave.

29 July 1979 (San Francisco)

Went to the Twin Peaks to meet Robby at 11:30 PM. He didn't show up until after midnight. We chatted a while about this and that, some nonsense that I can't recall now, when in walked this fellow, Sean, who worked with Robby. I always thought him attractive and pleasant enough, but never really knew him. He sat with us. I offered him my extra King Tut ticket as Robby didn't want to go with me the next day. He said "Yes" and I handed it to him, not wanting to make a big deal of it or demanding that he go with me. He thanked me with a kiss. After a few minutes I decided that I might want to go home with this man, so I pretty much threw myself at him.

After the bar closed we all went to Robby's flat on 16th Street for port. We were talking about music and I mentioned my love for Laura Nyro. Sean winced and when I asked him why, he said, "I was just fantasizing about a relationship with you, but I used to live with someone who played Laura Nyro all the time. I couldn't stand it again."

Later on I made some indiscreet comment about bondage or rough play, and Sean looked at me with renewed interest. Robby remarked that I shouldn't have said whatever I said because Sean would make me prove it. I perked up. As it turns out, Sean is very into SM and bondage.

I eventually ended up at Sean's place on Liberty Street. Since both of us were drunk, we tried getting some sleep before having sex. But we kept playing with each other, caressing and talking dirty.

"What do you like?"

"Everything," I said, thinking that he meant fucking and sucking.

"No you don't. If I hit you in the wrong place, you'd be so upset."

He had some hardware by the bed: handcuffs, rope, et cetera. I was a bit intimidated to see it but said only, "I'm just beginning to explore the rough side of it."

When we finally had sex the next morning, there was a lot of hitting, scratching, slapping and such. But no bondage. It all seemed to lack definition, like a piece of writing that rambled pointlessly on. I suspect now that he wanted me to establish limits while I was waiting for him to bring it up. Next time, if there is one, I'll bring the subject up, ask to be allowed to explore new horizons.[4]

The next day he made several references to my age (23 to his 29). He somehow thought me very young for the range of my experience. He also said that I was a pill but would grow out of it.

---

4 Two years later, while collared and on a leash, I would see Sean at my neighbor Larry's birthday party. Being collared, I only nodded to him and stayed close to my (then) Master. I never got another chance to thank him for that first lesson.

28 August 1979 (Provincetown)

The men here are beautiful. Not nearly so clonish as the Castro. A nice change. At tea dance at the Boat Slip I cruised a great beauty. He wasn't very tall, but lovely. He was slender, wearing only sneakers and running shorts. He had pale olive skin, curly hair all over his chest and torso, a neat little moustache, and beautiful wavy hair combed back (as is the latest style). I gave him a long hard stare, which he returned for a moment, then raised his chin in salutation and smiled. I returned the gesture, happy with the warmth of his response.

9 August 1979

They closed the A-House at 1:00 AM so I walked over to the beach behind the Boat Slip, which my little book[5] told me was cruisy. It was. I approached several people, all very nice, but no luck. One older man I cruised off and on hoping he'd approach me. He reminded me of Nick only not nearly as hot. One fellow explained to me about the bushes: There were only so many and people had to wait in line. People were sucking each other off pretty casually and I was missing it! I made my way over to the bushes and cruised the older man again. He had followed a pretty young blond all in white, and I followed him. The blond was a little putt-off, not knowing what was happening. The older guy asked me what I was up to.

"Cruising," I said.

"Really? I wish you had said that three hours ago!"

We got to my room at 3:00 AM, so it was only *two* hours. He was very nice, intelligent, a teacher (I think an art teacher) and he had a huge cock. He fucked me royal then sucked me off, spitting out the cum. We talked a bit and he left. I might see him on the beach again tonight.

31 August 1979 (Cherry Grove, Fire Island)

Getting here was not fun. I missed my flight from Provincetown to Boston because I had a hard time getting up with only two and half hours sleep. I was up late again fucking with Don (as his name turned out to be). Huge cock. It took both my hands to cover the shaft, still leaving the head. Also sucked a man in the bushes who was (again) older but very handsome. He couldn't get it hard but told me I'd have a good time, being very good at it.

---

5 *Damron's*, of course.

Don told me I was an exceptional lover and very beautiful; he liked the way I kissed.

After dinner tonight we went to hear some singer named Karen Akers at the Monster. Then we went to the Sandpiper to dance. Then to the meat rack in the Pines. After fooling around in the bushes at P'town, I was pretty much ready for what went on, but it was still all very new to me. The first thing I saw/heard was one man face-fucking another. The fucker was jockish looking in a sleeveless T-shirt. The cocksucker was a beautiful man we'd seen earlier at the Sandpiper. After the fucker came, he sucked-off the original sucker, who either pulled out early or came quickly. (I think the later.) Then they both pulled up their pants and wondered off in different directions.

Whenever two people started making it, others gathered around, feeling-up the two, pinching tits, maybe even sucking the cock of the cocksucker. One man sucked my cock but wasn't very good, so I pushed him away and pulled the fellow sucking his cock onto mine. I face-fucked both of them. After I came, he kept sucking. I finally lifted him up and left him with the first cocksucker. Later on I ran into Nick as he was sucking-off a lot of men while getting sucked himself. Face fucking definitely seems the norm. I looked for someone I'd like to suck. The guy I found was so drunk he couldn't cum. I left him undone. I did a lot of looking because I love to watch. I respect this sort of departmentalization because it's honest and to the point, no time wasted.

I decided later that I wanted to cum again so I waited for one cocksucker to finish another man and put his hand on my cock. After a moment of playing with my cock, he knelt down started sucking. He used poppers as I face-fucked him. A handsome, muscular Black man came along and started playing with my nipples. We kissed. I licked his face. (My first sexual contact with a Black man. I told Nick about him later and he said that he had done him too.) I realized that I wasn't going to cum because it was still too soon after my first orgasm, so I pulled out, stuck the Black man's cock in, and left them.

Then we went to the Cherry Grove meat rack, which is a dreadful maze of hillocks and vales. We saw some cocksucking, as usual, and felt-up a few cuties. We came on an SM trio. A three-way fuck, the middle number being a hunky Italian. I pinched the tits of the bottom. He gasped as I pinched harder, mesmerized by the pain. The top, and I suppose the Master, would occasionally slap them with a leather belt and they'd grown. Pretty serious stuff. A good time was had by all.

I can't recall another time when a Black man came onto me. Not only did I indulge the man last night, but also since my arrival I've been getting the cruise of death from another Black man. Don't like this other man at all. All he does is stare at me and look mean. Nick said right off that I shouldn't feel obligated to him as my only sexual partner, which is good because I don't.

4 September 1979 (Hackensack, New Jersey))

Fire Island is all it's reputed to be. Quite decadent. We went to the meat rack every night except last night because we had to wake-up early. I woke-up with the clap. First time and I'm very upset about it. Nick said that it's just a souvenir of Fire Island. Meanwhile, he has been put out of commission by a torn foreskin. One of the boys in the meat rack was pulling too hard on it, not realizing how sensitive it is.

Saturday night we were at the Cherry Grove meat rack until the sky began to grow light. I was invited home for a four-way, which was interesting if not terribly satisfying. My first experience with group sex. I came crawling in at 7:00 AM. Nick only laughed. Later, Nick woke me up making love to me. My mouth had opened to receive his tongue before my eyes had opened. I told him it was my favorite way to wake-up.

I also met a guy named Frank at the meat rack. He told me I was handsome, *et cetera*, but instead of sex we went for a walk on the beach.

21 September 1979 (Carmel, California)

One of Nick's games was to kiss me, inserting his tongue in my mouth, but withdrawing his mouth from mine if I responded in kind. Every time I returned the gesture he pulled away. It was a sort of power game, I think, and felt rather kinky at the time. I get excited just thinking about him. How that man can make me whimper.

21 October 1979

When I woke-up this morning, it was very cold. I could only think of how nice it would be to have another body there to share his warmth with me, to share my own with him. I then decided that I should fall in love again.

5 December 1979 (Hackensack, New Jersey)

Nick, Nick, Nick. I almost love him. We've had sex four times since I've been here, but only once when it was really exciting, really fun, to where I was making enough noise to worry Nick about disturbing the neighbors. But he took delight in my ecstasy. He mouthed my throat, nipples, navel, abdomen, and genitals; slapped me; pinched me. I went down on him, then fucked him. Again, I enjoyed eating the cum. I told him how much I enjoy sucking his cock, which is so rare for me.

6 December 1979

The first time we had sex on this visit I was too tired to really respond. He fucked me. The second time, I had to do all the work and I got the feeling that he was only doing it as a favor. The third was great. The last time, this morning, I started it. We only jerked ourselves off, like the second time. He spent most of his energy giving me very visible hickeys and throwing me around. But he had told me on Wednesday that he just wasn't horny, that he had been very horny the week before. Bad timing.

We also went to a backroom bar after the opera on Tuesday night, the Half Breed on 8th Avenue near 68th Street (I think). We stopped by for a drink. There we were in a Levi bar in our opera drag. We felt out of place. Nick had never been there before, either. There was a sign saying STABLES and pointing to stairway down. Nick went to pee and investigate. He was gone about ten minutes while I watched our things and felt progressively more uncomfortable. When he returned, he explained that there was, indeed, a backroom. My turn. I tripped down the dark stairs and moved about with deliberation through the half-lit and red-lit rooms before entering, cautiously, the dark room. Men leaned against the walls in the half-light watching me. I moved into the darkened room. Blind in the dark, I moved very slowly until I found a place to stand on the darkness' edge. I stayed there listening to the sounds of sex (slurping, breathing, the doing and undoing of pants). Soon someone came up, undid my zipper, took out my cock and sucked it. As I came I began to breath louder and make noise, knowing I'd get more attention. I did. Men stroked my tits and butt. It became a community effort. Like Fire Island. I loved it. When I returned Nick asked me if I'd gotten done. I told him "yes" of course. My experience at Fire Island's meat rack had trained me well in the attitude of stud, the dominant participant in depersonalized sex. Another new experience. So sleazy. The blackness made for an even more intense depersonalization. After sex, I simply put my clothes back together and walked back up the stairs. So very, very simple. Beats jerking-off.

13 December 1979 (Carmel, California)

Recollection about Nick: One night as we slept in spoons, his arms around me, I became semi-conscious long enough to be aware of him kissing the back of my neck and hugging me, holding me even closer to him for a moment. The next thing I was conscious of was his releasing his hold of me and laying apart from me on his back. Whether this happened instantly, a few minutes or even hours later, I don't know. Later, when awake, I wondered if he might have thought me, in his own sleepy mind, to be someone else.

31 December 1979

"I'm sure you've been in this position before."
I laughed. Said it was the best line I'd heard in a while.
Add Father Joey to the list. My latest lover is a Jesuit priest.
Nordic extraction, he said. Handsome and bearded. A gentle, but nonetheless enjoyable lover. Had only a single bed, however, and I had to go home and sleep alone after we had made love. Seduced me with a fine Leibfraumilch. I, already aware of his intent, helped him along. But we took our time. No hurrying at all. Wished we could have spent the night together. I love another body in the morning.

13 January 1980

Saw Joey again. He called me up on Thursday night saying that a meeting had been cancelled and he'd been freed for the evening. Could he come over? Of course. I opened a bottle of wine. He got physical. We moved to my room and made love.

I am mystified by it all. He told me how pleased he was to see me at Mass on Christmas Eve, how he enjoys "sharing it" with me. Me? It is a puzzle. I understand why others like me but not why he likes me. I can only think that it might be because I am so a part from him and his profession and his day-to-day life. Does that make me in some way exotic to him? Or merely safe?

4 March 1980 (San Francisco)

Safeway on Market Street. So many men. Better cruising than at a Greenwich Village laundromat. I want to live here.

Got my rocks off last night at the Locker Room peep shows. Got sucked-off while Chuck Connors queered-off on film. After I came, the man seemed somehow distraught. I left without a word. Good looking, though. I wouldn't have minded getting to know him.

6 March 1980

Met Robby at the Elephant Walk before lunch today, where I also saw Randy Shilts. He was better looking in person than on TV.

7 March 1980

Rolling in the gutter. A three-way with a leather-jacketed *hung* fellow named Jim and a pathetic, self-loathing alcoholic named Wayne. Met the two at the Locker Room. They both said that the place was trashy.

I said, "Yes, I love it!"

They didn't understand. Wayne had a bruise on his face; from an attacker or a trick, I don't know. Jim tried fucking me but wouldn't be gentle in his entry and I got angry. So I fucked Wayne while Wayne sucked Jim. Jim was hot but Wayne was pretty sad. I left before they'd finished, called a cab and took off. Came rolling in around 4:00 AM.

When I refused to let Jim turn me into a fuckhole, he just made me a partner in doing it to poor, pathetic Wayne. Wayne was very drunk and behaved like a popper junkie. He spilled the poppers (mine) all over Jim's bed.

It was all so sordid: "Take it like a man! Take it, bitch! Get on all fours because I'm gonna fuck you!"

16 March 1980 (Carmel, California)

Met a man named James Meade[6]. I like him.

24 March 1980

Much romance after the opera. We ate a cold supper I'd prepared ahead of time. Then we made love. Quietly at first. Very enjoyable. The nicest sex since my first night with Nick. There were a couple of times I wanted James to slap me hard across the ass, but was scared to ask him. I didn't think he'd be into it. He'd mouth my neck and ears, or my pelvis and torso, in a way that made me quiver and moan. I did the same to him and he accused me of having a mean streak. I told him he'd done the same to me.

"I didn't notice any resistance," he said.

"Only because I'm a masochist."

23 April 1980 (San Francisco)

Met Robby at the Twin Peaks where I had three Campari and sodas. I was drunk by the time we left. He asked me where I was going when I kissed him goodnight in front of his flat, then invited me to stay the night. I did. We hugged and kissed before falling off to sleep. Around dawn, when his roommate, Don, got up to get ready for work, we had sex. Wonderful. He fucked me and I came with only a little encouragement. Then we went back to sleep as Don left for work.

12 May 1980 (Carmel, California)

Julian. His place after work, after dinner and a lot to drink. We shared a joint.

"Are you going?"

"Yes, I'd better be off."

"Do you want to stay?"

"No, I... Was that a pass?"

---

6 An actor and singer, James had to move to Los Angeles shortly after this for a part in a Benjamin Britten opera. He eventually moved to San Francisco where he became a fixture in the local cabaret scene. We were close friends and lived in the same apartment building on Laguna Street for five years. Later, he and his husband would rent an apartment from us on Page Street. James died of AIDS there in 1988. For years I visited the church garden in San Francisco where his ashes were buried.

"Sort of, I...I'm not sure."

"You're not sure?" I put on my jacket and stood up, looking down on him still reclining. "When you're sure, let me know."

"That's just it. I won't be sure until I try it."

I felt very uncomfortable, wanting to but not sure of his motivations.

"It's not that I don't find you attractive. It's just that I don't know what you want or expect. But I would like to."

"Then take off your jacket and sit down."

I did. I laid on the floor and looked up at him sitting on the couch. I explained that I didn't want to get started and have him back out, nor did I want to spend the whole time wondering whether or not he was enjoying it and just going through with it for me. I also wanted to get a little more stoned. He opened a bottle of German wine. It was awful but we drank it Dutch courage.

"I hate sweet wine," he said.

I agreed.

He suggested a shower first, thinking that a good way to warm up.

"You see," he said, "I want to get fucked."

"Why? No, actually I do understand. I've read about you, about straight men wanting that."

"I've read about you, too. I want to see if I like it. Maybe I'll wake-up tomorrow morning and say, 'Gay sex is not for me.' Or maybe I'll say, 'Gay sex is wonderful! Let's do it again!'"

His Sheffield accent made me laugh.

"I wonder if I'm bisexual. I mean, I like men, gay men, and sometimes find men attractive. It's just that..."

We went to the shower. I touched him tentatively. His body is much nicer than I expected. His cock is lovely, large and uncut. We nuzzled each other. He fondled me roughly, but sensually. We kissed. He held me tight, tighter than I him. He ate my neck. (He *knew*. I'd told him that I love it.) He was rough but tempered. He bent down and sucked my cock.

"Was that good?" he asked.

"Wonderful. You've never done that before?"

"Never."

"You've a beautiful cock."

"Thank you."

I sucked his. The water splashed over me. As I gave him head, he washed my hair. It was getting intense.

"Do you still think I'll back out?"

He kissed me roughly once more. The hot water ran out and he turned the shower off. I checked to see if he was clean. He was. We toweled each other off and ran to his bed.

We wrapped ourselves in each other under a quilt on his bed, barely more than a cot. It was rough and exciting.

"Are you always this rough, or is it for my benefit?"

"Partly for your benefit. But I *am* a rough lover most of the time. I can be very tender, too, though…"

Then the time came to get down to business. Sucked me, played with my cock getting it good and hard.

I mounted him, rubbing my cock into his buttocks. This excited him and he wrapped his legs around me. I sat up and started to open him with a finger. He was tight. Like a virgin. (Of course!) When I got to the second finger he said that he needed to go to the toilet. I let him go even though I knew what was happening from my own experience, a trick the body plays on virgin butt holes. He came back and I knew at once that it was over.

"You're not really into it now, are you?" I asked.

"No. I guess not."

We laid in each other's arms. I tried to give him head to get him hard again so he could fuck me. No luck.

"I'm afraid I'm not into it at all now," he said. And then, "I'm sorry. I've led you on…"

"No, I…"

He explained that he hadn't been satisfied with his relationships (sexual, emotional) with women and hoped I was going to make it better, show him the light, make bells ring, and so on. We talked more. I already knew I'd be leaving, though. I never expected to be spending the night with him. I told him that it was all right.

"You didn't use me," I reassured him. "I've been used before and you didn't use me." I left him my number so he could call me should the need arise.

1 June 1980

Lethargic and in lust. His name is Yves and he is from Quebec. About my age, an architecture student on break, visiting friends in San Francisco after a semester in Mexico. And he draws. Today he drew me by the pool at his hotel. Handsome, sexy and very nice. He told me I was sexy when I spoke French, or sexi*er*. I eat flattery like French fries. We shared a joint this afternoon and I am still a little stoned. And tired. Crashed at 2:30 last night and had to wake up at 7:00 AM for work. We've yet to fuck in a bed. First in a car by the beach. Last night in a truck. So naughty. Never did it in vehicles before. What I won't do.

Met him Thursday night. He kept telling me I'm beautiful.

"*Bel homme.*" Or, "*C'est bon, David. C'est bon.*" Said that David was a beautiful name and that it fitted me. "You're skin is beautiful like that, so pale."

His accent is so sexy, as is he: Olive skin, growing a beard, beautiful green eyes. He smiles a lot, laughs. Appreciates. A wonderful, considerate lover.

But he has flown home.

11 June 1980

Last night Bob, Allen's ex-lover. (Still can't believe how Allen dumped him like that.) Some nervousness. Apologies.

"Don't let it bother you," I tell him.

"Next time it will be different," he says. "If you want to get back together again."

"Of course I do." I kiss him. "I enjoyed last night. If I told you I heard bells ringing you'd know that I was lying, but I have no ill will."

"I know," he interrupts. "My doctor said that it's just getting over hepatitis, that sex would be…"

I kissed him again.

Night before last Father Joey called. A film? Sure. After the movie Joey asked what I'd like to do next. Wine and cigars at his place? Sure. When there he asked if I wanted to spend the night. Why not? A good fuck, better than ever before with him. I was very relaxed. He pulled out of me and began to jerk off.

"Get back in there! Finish inside of me!"

I am not passive when passive. Nice sleeping with him. Left after breakfast feeling better about him than I have in ages.

1 October 1980 (San Francisco[7])

And Bob, the bouncer from the After Dark[8] in Monterey. Offered to love me "to death." I took him up on it. I thought him hot and he was/is. Like a picture by Tom of Finland: That brooding mustached face, the finely muscled body, brown silky hair covering the chest and torso. Large cock.

"You're making me cum," he said as I reached my own climax, his strokes battering home deep within.

The Joy of Fucking. We came together.

And another Bob on Sunday night. Went to the Jaguar for the first time, where we met. He came over to me in the video room and asked me home. I was whisked off in a sports car to Diamond Heights. Dare I complain?

He fucked me royal and well. I stayed the night.

"You have the distinction of being my first trick in San Francisco," I said.

"I'm not a trick."

I didn't ask.[9]

28 December 1980

I'm always astounded by the availability of sex in the City. I haven't had this much since my visit to Fire Island over a year ago. What is even more astounding to me is that I am almost always on the make. A day after tricking and I'm already looking for another man/more men. I usually just go to the Jaguar where I can fuck/get fucked as need be. Oddly enough, I find it harder to find a top man than a bottom[10].

---

7 I had just moved to San Francisco where I would live for the next 23 years. I only returned to Carmel to visit a few times after that, never enjoying my visits since I was never really happy the whole time I lived there. Moving back to San Francisco would always mark the real beginning of my life as an adult.

8 The After Dark was, at that time, the only gay bar on the Monterey Peninsula. The gay community, such as it was, was as small and incestuous as one might imagine, gossip being the primary recreation.

9 When I called Bob a week later and made a date with him, he stood me up without calling so I never spoke to him again. A few years later I noticed my boyfriend of the moment nodding to Bob on Castro Street. When I asked about him I learned that Bob had been with the same lover for over 10 years. So much for not being a trick.

10 Which indicates just how naïve I still was; I had no idea of how aggressive a bottom I would soon become.

One night at the Jaguar I found a wonderful top: Huge cock, all man. I screamed, "Fuck me! Fuck me!" and attracted something of a crowd. Now I'm horny as usual. Will hit the streets again tonight. Need/want a man to take me where I want to go.

5 January 1981

Got me some unhealthy love. Black gloved spankings and lots of dirty talk. And there may be something else to it: A boyfriend? His name is Jan and I first met him months ago with Robby. On Gay Day last summer I think. I've seen him around a few times since then, but we haven't really spoken much since. Than the other night I ran into him at the Twin Peaks with Robby's boyfriend Marc (who was mooning over Robby, who was mooning over Andy, who was fuming over Marc.) So Jan ended up coming home with me. Such a night! I was sore for days! Then again on Saturday.
"You want it?"
"Yes."
"Yes, *what*?"
"Yes, Sir!"
Smack!
"Thank you, Sir!"
And bent over his knee. Never have I felt so fulfilled.

14 January 1981

Just called Jan. Will be seeing him Saturday night. Talked dirty on the phone.
"Take out that gorgeous cock and stroke it!"
Last weekend I went out on my own. Ended up at the Jaguar. A pretty boy named Tom asked me to fuck him. I did, and without giving Jan a second thought. But I do think of him, or at least of our sex play, a lot: Fantasize of new, less wholesome games to play. I am so excited thinking about it now; I won't be able to sleep.

18 January 1981

Last night was so wild. And this morning. And this afternoon. I was ravished. The same sort of games only played with a great deal more earnestness than before. I was punished for my presumptuousness. Scolded and threatened. My ass, back and thighs slapped to a dull purple. I sobbed, clenched my teeth, bit a pillow.

I once gasped, "Please, Sir..." to be told, "You can take it!"

And I could. I did. New limits. My ass was fingered to stretch. I know he wants to fist fuck me, hopes to slowly lead me to it. Once I cried tears because I was afraid that I'd done wrong, but it was all right. He made it (or me) all right again.

I screamed: "Fuck me, Sir! Please fuck me, Sir! I can take it, Sir! Give it to me, Sir, give it all to me! I can take it, Sir!"

Once he asked whose ass he was fucking.

"Mine, Sir."

"*What?!*"

"It's your ass, Sir. All yours. You can fuck it whenever you want to, Sir."

He did. Drove me wild.

This afternoon I laid on his bed, my feet up, with a robe of his loosely wrapped around me; a pose I've taken for years that no one has ever responded to before. He ravished me, fucked me for the third time. Easy at first but so hard at the end when I begged him to shoot. So hot. Asked if I had pleased him.

"Yes."

Would he continue to train me?

"Yes."

His pubes had been shaved.

24 January 1981

My birthday party.

James: "David hasn't been spanked yet. He needs his birthday spanking."

Everyone Else: "Oh, yes."

Me: "No."

Larry grabs my arms. I want to resist but don't.

Jan: "Yes."

I can't deny him. He bends me over his knee counting to 25 with an extra slap and a kiss to grow on.

Then on Thursday night I went out and ended up at the Jaguar (sort of by accident, but not really.) This time I wanted to top but everyone's hands were all over my ass. I eventually came. Was sucked three times, the last so good I finally came (in seconds). When I got home I undressed and, feeling a little blue, laid on my bed in the nude contemplating masturbation when the phone rang. It was Jan. I was overjoyed.

He apologized for not staying the night of my birthday party but wanted me to come over now. I looked at the clock, 9:00 PM. I thanked him for sharing my birthday with me.

"I'd like to give you another spanking."

Of course. We agreed that I'd be there in half an hour.

I arrived five minutes late, already afraid that he would discipline me for my tardiness. He opened the door and I was at once taken aback. The apartment was candle lit, otherwise completely dark, and he was in leather (save for his jockstrap). Completely in leather.

I entered and just stood there. Said hello. Wanted to touch him but didn't dare make a move. I went to the table and removed my jacket, laying it on the table with my umbrella. He approached, held me gently and kissed me. How was my day?

"Fine. Thank you, Sir."

"Happy birthday."

"Thank you, Sir."

Then he told me that I could take off my clothes and leave them on the chair. I did as I was told.

He went into the bathroom and made some bathroom noises. He came back to where I stood naked. Held me again.

"You've showered?"

"Yes, Sir."

"Have you douched?"

"No, Sir."

"I think you should."

"Yes, Sir."

"Have you ever douched before?"

"No, Sir."

"Okay. Everything will be fine if you do what you're told."

"Yes, Sir."

The bathroom was steamy. He glistened in his leather.

The enema was not so gruesome as I feared nor as pleasurable as I had hoped. He asked if I was full. I said, "Yes."

"Does it want to come out?"

"Yes, Sir."

"How is that going to happen?"

"I don't know, Sir." (I didn't!)

Something Sensational to Read in the Train

"You're going to have to beg, aren't you?"
I tried begging, poorly.
"I don't think you mean it."
I was getting uncomfortable.
"Please, Sir, please! Please let me release the water, Sir!"
"All right."
I released the water. He washed me off and stuck the hose back up my ass. The second time I was filled even fuller, which I didn't hold all of when he pressed into my abdomen with his fist. As punishment, I had to take third, very full bag that I had to fill myself.
"What sort of punishment am I going to give you?"
I knelt down in the tub trying hard to hold all the water in.
"I don't know, Sir."
"Fantasize."
"You'll whip me with the belt, Sir, and make it hurt more than I want."
"No, I don't think more than you want."
I cried out in pain.
"What's wrong?" he asked coolly.
"It hurts. The water wants to come out. But I can hold it, Sir. I can hold it as long as you want, Sir."
I was told to release it. I did. He put his boot on the edge of the tub.
"Kiss my boot." I did with great pleasure.
"Lick it."
I did so with equal pleasure.
"You're going to lick all of my leather aren't you?"
"Yes, Sir. May I start with the chaps, Sir?"
"You're not done with the boot yet are you?"
"No, Sir."
"You haven't even touched the other side."
"No, Sir."
Again, I did as I was told.
Then he told me to clean myself up, dry off and tell him when I was ready. When I was clean and dry again, I opened the door again and told him. I was told to bring in the candles from the bathroom. I did, placing them on the bookcase as told. Then I licked his other boot and the left side of his chaps. I was told to stop licking the leather and to start on the jockstrap, to get it "good and wet." Then I was allowed to take his cock out with my hands. I kissed the head.

"Did I say you could do that?"

"No, Sir. Please forgive me, Sir."

I was allowed to kiss his balls, then suck them. Then the head of his cock, then all of it. He forced my head down on it, making me choke. Asked why I was choking. I apologized saying I didn't know how to swallow such a big cock. At some point (which I can't remember now) he started to whip my ass with his belt while his dick was still in my mouth. I took it well, savored it even, until his lashes reached under my buttocks to my balls. I cried out involuntarily.

"Whose ass is this?"

"Yours, Sir."

"Then why are you pulling it away?"

"It hurts, Sir. I'm sorry, Sir."

He continued the whipping and I, no longer relishing the pain, called out, cried, and continued sucking his dick.

I can't remember exactly how it happened, but he was standing over me again. Not knowing what to do, or if I'd displeased him, I began sucking his cock. He knelt down next to me, held me and asked if I was okay. I held back a sob. I was horrified and in agony.

"You...! You...!"

"Go ahead, cry. Tell me."

"I'm frightened. You...."

"I took you farther than you wanted to go."

"Yes. You slapped my balls with the belt. It hurt so but I wanted to take it. I wanted to take all of your pain, Sir."

We laid down together.

"Am I your Master?"

"Yes, Sir."

"If I'm your Master, do you know what that makes you?"

"Your slave, Sir."

"A good slave tells his Master everything, doesn't he?"

"Yes, Sir."

"A bad slave is a slave left on the wayside. He isn't even a slave."

I held him tighter.

"Now I can't stretch your limits if you don't tell me, can I?"

"No, Sir."

I refilled his wine glass, prepared and lit a new cigar for him. Then, as ordered, sucked his cock, almost gagging. He must have forced my head down for me to choke like that, but I don't remember. We got into a 69 position. I sucked his cock as he spanked and rimmed me.

It must have been about now that he told me to take off his boots. I did so lovingly, kissing the boots as I put them carefully aside. Then he fucked me. When we changed positions (as is his wont) my ass disengaged from his cock. This displeased him. I hung my head. He ordered me to lay down on my tummy. He grabbed his belt and started snapping it.

"What does that mean when you hear the belt snap like that?"

"That you're going to whip my ass, Sir. Because I need it, Sir."

Again, I enjoyed the pain. He pulled out my cock and balls from underneath me where they could be gotten at easily. He never touched them. Trust. I began to flinch, asked him to switch cheeks.

"I'm not done with this one yet."

A few more strokes. It really began to hurt again.

"Why are you flinching? Do you need for me to stop again?"

"Yes, Sir."

We laid down again and he held me.

"This is the second time I've had to tell you, now. Tell me when you need to stop. A good slave tells his Master."

"Yes, Sir. I'll try to be a good slave, Sir."

"You're not a slave yet."

"No, Sir."

We fell asleep in each other's arms. We awoke a little later. I helped him out of his chaps, kissed them and his vest as I laid them aside. As I laid in his arms again he said,

"You'll get your cock and cum later."

"Yes, Sir. Goodnight, Master."

Later he woke me in the usual way, his fingers up my ass, and fucked me, cumming before he meant to. He held me, his cock still up my ass, as I jerked off. He apologized for cumming so soon.

"But you got me so excited I couldn't help it. Like you're supposed to."

"Thank you, Sir."

"Thank *you*."

At some point during the night, while I was on my knees, he wrapped the belt around my throat. I was excited and terrified. I've a long-standing phobia of being choked. Later on I, sobbing, asked him if he'd please not to do it anymore.

He agreed, saying, "You need to tell me, or how else can I know?"

Then I kissed the belt, again with great pleasure.

The next morning my ass had bruises and welts. It's still bruised. Yesterday it hurt to sit down. He called me last night to check on me before he left for the weekend. He said he'd call me tomorrow. I miss him. I want him. I'm not in love, though. I trust him: Something akin to love.

28 February 1981

I met Randy Shilts a week ago at the Brig.
Shilts: How're you doing tonight?
Me: Just fine.
Shilts: Just fine, huh?
Me: Yeah.
Shilts: Yeah? Children starving, social unrest and turmoil in the world, and you're just fine?
Me: Yeah. I *was* going to say how much I enjoyed your last article in *Christopher Street*. But fuck you, you arrogant sonuvabitch.
Shilts:I didn't think you knew who I was.

From then on things were fine. He spilled my soda and I mopped it up with my handkerchief.
Shilts:What color is that?
Me:Dark blue.
Shilts:What side was it on?
Me.The right.
Shilts:You know what that means?
Me.Of course.
Shilts:That's the side I'm interested in.
Me:Yeah?
Shilts:Know what I like? I like to tie boys up and spank them 'til they call me Daddy and Sir. I bet that turns you off.
Me:No.
Shilts:No? Can I buy you a drink?

I proceeded to explain that I'd gotten a note from the clinic on Friday. (I didn't know yet that it was a follow-up appointment. I had just assumed the worse.)
Me:So I've got something and I may have given it to my Master.
Shilts:You've got a Master? How do you feel about having a Master?
Me:I like it. It fulfills a need.
Shilts:I'm a Master sometimes…

It was arranged that I would call him. I did. He remembered me. He came over last night bringing his own beer. I called him Daddy and Sir, and sucked his balls and cock, and let him spank me, whip me, tie me up and fuck me. It was fun but lacked the intensity of sex with Jan. As he left he told me that he was one of the most interesting people I'd ever meet. He also said he'd call me, that we'd get together again.[11]

26 April 1981

Jan as regularly as before. When I serve him I seem to reach new ecstasies, new levels of understanding. SM has given me myself by removing the clutter. Jan once described it as stripping away all the layers to who we really are. That in itself is almost enough to partake in serving a Master. There is so much involved, so many layers of experience and understanding, ways of interpreting the interactions and dynamics of sexual slavery. Part of it is having a clear definition, which for a period of time can be completely fulfilled without reservation or fear. This fulfillment of a defined self is cause for rejoicing. How often is one allowed to be one's self, to fulfill a significant part of one's own needs through another human being? In this there is a type of completeness.

I have not served my Master for some time and have started to become anxious. I need his lash, his leather, his hand, the voice that calls me "cocksucker," "slave," and "fuckhole". I exalt in it, for in it is my power, my strength: He cannot so define me without my consent.

7 April 1981

Jan called. I started off the conversation being off-hand and flippant, ended with "Sir"s and "thank you"s. Quivering and undone. He knows what his Mastery does to me. Jan has grown a beard and it's very handsome, gray and black. I'll feel his beard on Thursday night.

---

11 I called him a few weeks later but he never returned my call so I didn't pursue him. I called his office a year or so later, while he was still at the *San Francisco Chronicle*, to ask him about an article that had quoted him in *California Magazine*. I had no reason then to think that he remembered me or recognized my voice. Several years later, when his celebrity had reached it's zenith and half the people in the room were fawning over him, he sat next to me at some function or other. I don't know if he recognized me then as I was chatting with a friend (about the Oz books, of all things) the whole time and never spoke to him. If he remembered me then, or wanted to say something about our one date, I'll never know.

9 June 1981

Garth is a sweet, hot Daddy, whom I originally met through Jan some months ago. I've been hot for him for some time, since I first met him. We sat across from each other on the Muni one afternoon, quite by accident, and I started to flirt with him.

"I like your jacket. Well, I like tweeds. Actually I noticed your jacket before I noticed you."

The I heard Jan's voice, "David, is that anyway to talk?"

Failed attempt. But at Tom's party, on Friday night before last, all went well. I let him (such sacrifice!) get me stoned, then tripped with him.

"I'll stay with you the whole way," he said.

I *loved* it. And he was a lot of fun in bed. I almost told him, but didn't, that I'd wanted him for a while, that I had planned on nabbing him that evening.

At breakfast he said, "You've been toilet trained within an inch of your life." I guess the New England Puritan still comes through.

Jan and I had a scene last Thursday evening. It was very intense, very exhausting, taking everything out of me. I wanted to leave afterwards, to go home, and to spend the night alone to rekindle my energies. But I spent the night with him feeling desperate. I slept fitfully. After our scene he saw how spacey I was, treated me gently, served me tea and custard pie, kept asking me how I was, gave me seconds, shared himself with me. But all this was not enough: I was depleted. Come morning, I asked him not to whip me, to stop playing with my asshole. He did fuck me, though, and I enjoyed it. He even asked me if I wanted to be fucked. As always I did, but I couldn't take anything else. New accoutrements were tried: my collar and leash, tit clamps. There was a confrontation over the tit clamps. He had not warned me about how painful it would be when he removed the clamps. As the blood rushed back to the nerve endings, I bit hard on the towel he had put in my mouth, held on tight to him, like a vice as he ordered me. I whimpered, was angry, and had not understood then that it was inevitable. He became angry, accused me of being distrustful, and asked me if I wanted to leave. I apologized then, and again later on when I could put into words how shocking the experience had been. Even now, though, I feel unresolved. How can I trust me if he doesn't explain? Is my trust in him to include and accept what is left unexpressed? If so, such a request is gargantuan.[12]

11 June 1981

The man, Mick, was pleased with me. (He must really like me: He bought me a slave collar on our first date.) Took me out to show me off, rearranging my jacket before we went into the Brig. I got to wear his motorcycle jacket, which fit me well but still felt too large, like a child in one of Daddy's shirts. I did look good in it, though. Sweet leather.

I am not to be his slave for a while. I am just his fuckhole until he finishes training me. He said that I'd been much better trained than he had anticipated, that it was easier to call me slave than he thought it would be. Called me pretty, made me feel cared for. I felt very calm at the end of the scene. He brought me home around midnight.

24 June 1981

Last night at Hamburger Mary's: I was paying the bill at the bar. The bartender/cashier handed me my change with one hand and pulled at my slave collar with the other.

"Who's the lucky man?"

I nodded to the dining room and said, "He's in there."

The bartender smiled and so did I. When I sat down again I told Mick. He suggested that we show off and we went into the bar. I told him which bartender (blue tank, black leather armbands, cute) it was.

When I got our drinks, the bartender said, "That's him with the hat?"

"Yes."

"You're both hot."

I told Mick, swollen with pride.

---

[12] This was the last time we played, as I would shortly meet my next Master. This was a choice I came to regret when the new Master proved to be unworthy of both the name and me. It would be a while before I realized how much I had come to love Jan, and to suspect that he had held me in some affection as well. Jan was always very kind to me whenever we met after this, and I have always been grateful to him for all he taught me. I'm glad now that I thought to thank him a few years later.

27 September 1981

Last night Mick fucked me long and hard, the way I like it. It was the first time he fucked me in over a month. And he did it so well.

28 March 1982

Met a man last week named Steve. He was well hung and long lasting, talked dirty and played Daddy. I was a good boy. He worked my nipples like no one had ever done before, giving me pleasure/pain like I've never known. He'd fuck me until he was close to cumming, then withdraw and kiss me and/or work my tits. This went on for an hour and a half. Heaven. When it was over, he hopped out of bed like it was nothing. I laid on the bed, spent. He wants to get together again, to do something "besides just fuck."[13]

31 May 1982

The man of my dreams was at the Great Tricycle Race. About my height in boots, with tremendous shoulders, a lush but beautifully trimmed beard, full leather, a pierced left nipple, and covered with soft silky black hair – chest, shoulders, arms. I couldn't help but stare. There was a gentleness about him that was reflected in his manner of touching other men, firmly, calmly, just like a Daddy would. I would have licked his boots then and there. Fantasy material. Too beautiful for words[14].

---

13 We never did.

14 I never saw this man again except in my mind's eye. With the addition of a tattoo, he is the man I called Carl in my first published story, **Cutting Threads**.

24 August 1982

I met Brad[15] at the Cauldron two Saturdays ago. We played, had a good time. He fucked me, spanked me. And fucked me again. So I told him that I'd like to play with him again. He said, "Sure," that the next weekend (last weekend) would be good for him because his lover would be out of town. I played it cool but gave him my number. When he called on Tuesday I verified that he was involved in an open relationship and that our liaison would in fact not be clandestine.

On Saturday last I arrived at his apartment in the big building on Duboce and Church Streets at 9:00 PM. He greeted me in full leather. Very exciting. His beard is lush and beautiful. He is muscular and furry. His left nipple is pierced and he has a Chinese Dragon tattooed on his left shoulder. We talked for a while before playing. His leather pants had a codpiece. I licked the codpiece and then, when he removed it, sucked his cock. I did my best to give him head, going down as far as I could and doing my best to control the gag reflex. Once, when I choked, he pulled my head back and kissed me. He fucked me while I was tied to the bed.

"You like Daddy's cock up your ass, don't you boy? You like feeling Daddy's leather?"

"Yes, Daddy, yes. Fuck me please, Daddy. Thank you, Daddy."

The session was short and sweet, but lacking intensity, for which he apologized, explaining that he had been studying all day. We sat around and talked, eventually getting back to sex and fetishes. I got turned-on and asked him to play with my hole while I got off. He happily obliged. As he slipped in a finger, I handed him his leather cap. He smiled and put it on.

While he played with my hole he said things like, "Cum for your old man. Let me see you cum."

He poked my prostate right on target. So I stopped jerking on my cock and let it happen. I came like rockets. Then I asked him to notify my next of kin.

---

15 A poet and music critic, Brad was one of the handsomest, and hottest, men I ever played with. I later learned that he had once been roommates with my friend Cynthia Slater's former lover, author and sex educator Dossie Easton; and that his partner, another David, was a regular playmate of my office coworker, Mark (who died in the late 1980s) who was also an old friend of Cynthia's. Dossie (whose home in the Santa Cruz Mountains I would later describe in my story **The Center of the Maze**) and Cynthia were both close friends of my future Daddy and husband David Lourea. All of which goes to show just how very incestuous San Francisco truly is.

3 October 1982

Saw Brad in front of Safeway today. Some men look better by moonlight. I almost didn't recognize him but for his beautiful tattoo.

Meanwhile, at the Catacombs[16] Friday night, I played only with Bear. Had a great time. Was assertive, communicative, and allowed the scene to be fluid. We were the only ones in the playroom at first but eventually acquired an audience that included women and straight men getting off on us. I was taken where I wanted to go, and all so seamlessly. I felt so safe and content when it was over that I was close to tears. Felt high from the intensity of the scene, from the eroticism of it. Got to bed around 2:30 AM and woke-up two hours later with a raging hard-on. I absolutely *had* to jerk-off then, and again when I was woke-up at 10:00 AM. *Had* to. Will play with Bear again in the near future.

6 December 1982

The Catacombs again on Friday. Played with Guido. He tied me very securely, arms and hands, bent over the motorcycle in the playroom, and spanked me all over with his hands and *my* belt.

"I like hands and belts," I'd said.

"I didn't wear a belt tonight."

"I did."

He left several bruises, which I (as always) feel rather proud of.

---

16 The Catacombs was the premiere SM/fisting club in San Francisco for many years, going through at least three locations and two owners before finally closing in 1983. The Catacombs was now at its final location on Shotwell Street. To go to the Catacombs one had to be invited or answer the one ad that was placed in the queer papers each year – and even then one was thoroughly grilled before being accepted. My friend at the time, professional dominatrix Cynthia Slater, hosted monthly parties there and invited me. I knew I had arrived at the Catacombs when, a year or so later, mentioning my name was enough to get invited to the club. Robert Mapplethorpe had already taken Cynthia's portrait by this time, a fact I remained ignorant of until the late 1990s. We eventually had a falling out (as she did with many of her friends over the years), something that I've long regretted. Cynthia died of AIDS of in 1989.

Then I played with David Lourea[17], a smaller dark man who, it turned out, has a wife: Bisexual. Our scene started around ass play but ended-up centered on boot licking. He fucked me in such a position that I could lick his boots while he was plugging my hole.

"I'm cumming, Sir. May I cum, Sir?"

"Look my boot harder, harder!"

I came, beautifully.

Then: "Kiss the boot good-bye now, like you mean it."

He told me later that he had never been so excited by having his boots licked before. I told him that he had never been with anyone who enjoyed bootlicking as much I do before. Exceptional play.

Also got to watch my friend Neal[18] get into a very heavy whipping scene with David, one wherein a third party joined the scene without permission. I hovered around until the scene's climax, and then ran to get ice to put on the welts. David helped me administer the ice. I was concerned because I was afraid Neal wouldn't give the signal to stop when it was time. I spoke to him later and discovered that I was right: He was punishing himself. I sensed this already because I had done the same thing when Jan was training me.

5 January 1983

Last night, instead of writing or doing laundry or returning phone calls, I went to the Cauldron. I clicked with a man named Cameron, good looking but hefty, with a fairly new beard. He worked my tits, sucked my cock, kissed me, fucked me, slapped me around a little and kissed me some more. Lots of kissing. Really nice. After we parted I sought out others, or tried to, to play with but never really clicked again. I got more off on watching one Master in particular (who reminded me of Bear) doing his boy than I did on anything else. I was envious of the boy.

---

17 This is the first time I met the man who would eventually become my spouse and Sir for almost eight years. I had a crush on him almost from the beginning, a crush that I kept in check whenever we met or played together. It was another two years, after he and his wife divorced, before he caught me between boyfriends and began to court me. Until he asked me out to dinner I was completely unaware that he had been just as smitten with me the whole time. He died in 1992 leaving behind hundreds of mourners of all ages and descriptions. I've always felt especially grateful to have been his partner and boy during those years. He taught me more about life and love than can be put into words.

18 Neal was an exceptionally beautiful man who modeled for Colt Studios. Always a pleasure to be around, I missed him when he left San Francisco. Last I heard he was living in Los Angeles.

20 September 1983 (San Diego)

On Friday night I went out to the Loading Dock wearing a leather vest, black hankie and slapper on my left, and met a handsome man named Rich Jamieson[19]. We went from there to the Hole. When he asked me where I wanted to go next, I asked him, "Do you want to play?" Yes. So I played with his nipples and we kissed, locked mouths. Oh, for a cannibal's kiss! When we got to his place I showed him my toys: riding crop, slapper, tit clamps. I topped. Put him in a collar, a first for him. Used his handcuffs on him. Put on my new gloves. He ate my jock strap, sucked my cock, licked my boots, took my pain, asked for more, and got fucked. When I took the collar off of him, and after we had showered, he fucked me. His cock is *enormous*. *Hurt!* But no complaints.

I spent the night with him in his apartment on Loma Portal, the fan on all night drawing in cooler air from the window and circulating it softly over us, our bodies covered by a single sheet. Beautiful image. The next morning he told me that his roommate had been standing by the door jerking-off while we fucked.

4 October 1983 (San Francisco)

I want to describe Rich in more detail. Particularly his face. Half Polish, he has what he calls a pug nose, one I find very cute, even handsome, in profile: Straight, up-turned and present. He's freckled everywhere, even his lips, and has pale skin that burns then tans. Beautiful coloring. His hair is dark with red highlights from the sun. His beard and moustache are auburn with brown and blonde. Predominately dark red. His body hair changes color over his body. A part of his pubic hair is red, the rest brown. He is nothing less than handsome.

But what I really want to describe is a certain expression of his. Whenever we kissed our cannibal kiss, he'd sometimes pull his head, lower his chin, and give me something like a child's sly smile. I've been thinking of that expression for a few days now and I guess I've only just realized how charmed I am by it.

---

19 One of the great, but unrequited, loves of my life, Rich Jamieson was a talented artist as well as Mr. San Diego Leather 1985. That we were both equally unwilling to move the other's city was just one of the obstacles that kept us from taking the plunge; the other being his need for monogamy. He died in 1989, leaving a void in the lives of his two children and many others.

22 October 1983

Brad last night. Used me as a footstool, a fantasy of mine that I'd never mentioned. Had only told him that I needed humiliation. Good sex as well. Used lambskins, which felt very close to natural. He spent the night with me as his lover had a date over at their place.

1 November 1983

Rich arrived on Friday night.
I put the collar on him Saturday night. He was disobedient.
"Whose ass is this?"
"Yours, Sir."
"Whose cock is this?"
No answer.
"Whose cock is this?"
I squeeze it harder. No answer.
"Whose cock is this?"
I squeeze even hard on it. He gasps in pain.
"Yours, Sir."
"Why didn't you answer me the first time, boy?"
I'm still squeezing his cock.
"I don't know, Sir."
I spit in his face and roll him over onto his stomach.
"Count, boy."
And three very hard swats with the length of the riding crop.

He told me later that he wanted to see what would happen, that when he saw how angry I was he became frightened. I then explained to him that punishment might involve having the collar taken from him – rejection. He promised that it would never happen again, that he was sorry.

Very hot. Very real. The exhilaration of ownership. And he is so hot. I suppose I'm in love.

15 November 1983

The moments with Rich that I most enjoy remembering are the quiet ones. In San Diego we were laying on the couch listening to Billie Holiday for a while, his head on my lap. Once here, while he was collared and sitting between my knees as I sat on the couch. We were taking a break in the scene listening to Culture Club's new record. Him naked and mine.

18 November 1983

I think it first all came into focus when I was 11 or so, when my best friend Leigh and I went to see **Wild Angels** with Peter Fonda. Much of it, like rape, was implied rather than shown, and I was simultaneously frightened and excited by it, beyond anything I could remember. Soon, quite by accident at first, I started to jerk-off, and then to jerk-off wearing black leather gloves, fantasizing about violent sex with men who were virile, hairy; with moustaches, sideburns and stubble. And tattoos. And then men raping me. For years I buried it all: Loving men, SM. I wouldn't think about the later for years, not until Robby slapped my buns, got a little rough. Then I wanted more, craved it, though it would be two and a half more years before Jan brought me out into SM, slowly and with careful deliberation. I will always be grateful to him. A Master, I eventually learned, isn't the monster I was afraid he'd be, but only a part of me, someone to love and cherish, a means of coping with internal dramas and demons.

26 November 1983 (San Diego)

Spent last night with Rich. We cuddled all night long on his waterbed. His left tit is pierced. It will look even prettier with a gold ring in it. The pain is still there in his eyes and I wanted to ease it. "You need lots of affection tonight, don't you, boy?" "Yes, Sir." I held him tightly. Then I made love to him, fucked him both last night and this morning. Left marks on his neck. I always feel the need to mark him.

"Now everyone will know you have a Daddy who takes care of you."

23 December 1983

After Christmas shopping today I stopped to see a leather porn flick at a porn shop on Polk Street. Always a pleasure. Was at the Catacombs last Friday night. After I topped Chuck, whipping him within an inch of his life to the **Hallelujah Chorus**, Ta whipped me, forcing me to beg on my knees so everyone could hear:

"Please, Mistress, I've been bad and need to be beaten." Left a lot of pretty marks. The next day at Cynthia Slater's tree-trimming party, she and I went into the bathroom where I dropped my pants and showed her the marks. She liked them. She keeps calling me a sweetheart and a good boy.

"So responsive. I like the way you yell."

Chuck called me the next day to say that his fanny was a checkerboard from my riding crop.

4 March 1984

Topped Mick for the first time last night.
He said, "You've become the person I always wanted you to be."
And afterwards, "You're a hot top."
I knew that already but only thanked him.

17 March 1984

Last night I did the Catacombs with Mick. Had a good time. Gayle and her girlfriend we're there. These women played *mean*. Mick is not so outstanding as a bottom. We play differently than we did before (role reversal aside). He asked to be tied-up, gagged, blindfolded and abandoned. I was happy to oblige. Used my new sign: DO NOT TEASE, TORMENT, TOUCH, FEED OR SPEAK TO THE ANIMAL WITHOUT ITS MASTER'S PERMISSION!!! I got a host of compliments on it. A *hot* party. Fucked Chuck again – this time with a condom, which I felt better about. Called me a "real man" again and complimented me on my prowess. Yes, I *am* good sex.

19 May 1984

Met Yoni at the Eagle after answering his personal ad. I figured he wasn't husband material in about 10 minutes. So, when he kissed me at the Brig and forced me to my knees to lick his codpiece, I accepted his decision that I needed to be tied-up and went home with him. If I thought there had been the potential for a real relationship, I'd have demurred last night and held out for more when I knew him better.

Gags, blindfolds, masks and hoods are his specialties. Safe sex, whips and hot wax. Such a jaded boy, I noticed that there were two different whips used on me without even looking. He gave me a ride home at 2:30 AM. A gentleman.

While I'm on the subject, I also played with Allan Bérubé[20] from up the street for the first time a few weeks ago. Very hot, twisted. We went to see a straight dominatrix porno film that was produced by a woman. A lot of fun and very funny. Called **Smoker**. Then we came here and played. A Daddy scene. Cock and ball torture. Whenever I reached a new level of pain, I said, "Thank you, Daddy." And when I needed him to stop, I kissed him. Very powerful, very effective play.

2 July 1984

After the Parade and going to the dance to see Sylvester with Cary (just like old times) I went to the Academy. Did a very short Daddy scene. Didn't get his name. It could never be repeated, anyway. Safe sex: A condom, no rimming (I refused him the pleasure of "kissing Daddy's ass hole") though he begged for it. Proud of myself for sticking to safe sex without breaking the rhythm of the scene.

19 July 1984

Out with Yoni. We capped off the evening with a little public humiliation. He put a collar on me, took me into the Brig, bought me a Calistoga, told me to stand-up by a pillar and walked away for a few minutes. Men cruised by me, looking me over. I kept my eyes towards the floor. A major turn on.

28 July 1984

Played with Allan Bérubé again on Thursday. We had never bothered to establish safe words before and had never needed them. This time we did. Not knowing better, his mistook "Please stop, Daddy" with "more, more, more." I called out "Allan!" and he stopped and held me, untied me. Apologies. We talked about it and he encouraged me to cry. While I was genuinely frightened

---

20 I'd first met Allan Bérubé, albeit briefly, in 1980 at the Unitarian Church where was giving the talk that would eventually become *Coming Out Under Fire*. I met him four years later at the first Safe Sex Seminar on record. It was held at the Cauldron, and Allan arrived with two leather dykes, Gayle Ruben and her then lover. I knew that any man who attends a leather function with two dykes was the kind of man that I wanted to know and so, with my usual forwardness, I approached him. We played a couple of times, but more importantly, he encouraged my writing and introduced me to other writers. His recent demise was a great loss to the community as a whole.

and allowed myself to be pushed over the edge, felt betrayed and even violated, I also felt closer to him in the end.

When it was all over I said, "I still want to be your boy, Sir."

"Fucking pervert."

30 October 1984

I find leather and SM of increasing importance to me, as well as my identity as a leather man. I'm reading Mains' *Urban Aboriginals*[21]. The further I read, the more I see SM as valid, as my own experience. Also borrowed Grumley's *Hardcore* from Cynthia Slater. Such are my interests. Also, as I play more, I see it as more and more essential to my emotional well-being. I crave the sensations of power, of pleasure and pain.

4 November 1984

Did Folsom Street with Pete Hopkins[22] on Halloween. Out until late. Felt like who I was/am: A leather man, and a hot one at that. I asked Pete why we weren't lovers. He said that he was afraid of me, afraid that I'd release what he wanted to keep locked-up: He'd rather stay frustrated. Last night I went to a party at the SM House (*nee* the Catacombs) with Yoni. He left pretty marks with a braided cat-of-nine-tails. Feels so good to submit. Lots of humiliation, both there and later at the Brig. I was very happy by the time he dropped me off.

14 November 1984

On Saturday night I went to the California Motorcycle Club Carnival Dance on Pier 45, again with Pete. Very hot energy. So-so music. Beautiful men. Lots of leather. We wore ours and were very hot (we thought.) We each played with strangers in the depths of the warehouse. I got off on the sleaziness of it all, but kept to safe sex. Slapped one man around as he licked my boots.

---

21 My first published story, **Cutting Threads** appeared in the same issue of *Drummer* that had an excerpt from *Urban Aboriginals*. When I met Mains at a book signing and shared with him our very tenuous connection, he was very generous and wished me well with my future writing. David Lourea and I played with him occasionally at the SM House not long after that. I've always been grateful for the encouragement he gave me as a writer.

22 Pete was one of my best friends for years. He committed suicide in 1992 after his second bout with an AIDS-related illness. Our never having been lovers mystified everyone, including us. I still miss him.

Loved the attention this brought. It was all so *madrugada*[23]. Dancing and playing until 4:00 AM. And the decadence of it all: I waited for a bolt of lightening from above.

23 November 1984

Lunched with Yoni. Such an enigma. I find him handsome, charming even, and more so than before. We talked about dominance and submission, safe sex, group play, altered states. Play in general. I told him how deeply I felt connected to him at the SM House a few weeks ago. He concurred. The conversation made me want to play. Then he called me not half an hour after he'd dropped me off here.

"I get the impression that you're ready for something more."
"Yes, Sir."
"Yeah, I think you better call me 'Sir.' You'll be hearing from me."[24]

---

23 A delicious Portuguese word I'd come to love, meaning "the time between midnight and dawn." It eventually became the title of my first book.

24 By the time he got around to calling me again I was already dating, and madly in love with, David Lourea. I saw Yoni socially a few times after that but we never played again.

An Apparent Proximity

This is neurosis in a nutshell:
the miscarriage of clumsy lies about reality.
– Ernest Becker

It's so easy to blame the other when a love affair ends badly, perhaps even inevitable, but with Mick it was perfectly justified.

In my twenties, I had already had numerous love affairs (most of them embarked upon as much out of habit as out of a persistent desire to be in love) that lasted a few weeks to a few months. I was prone to short, intense love affairs that left me physically exhausted, emotionally drained, and strangely satisfied. There was little I enjoyed more than a few nights spent listening to Billie Holiday and Laura Nyro in the dark of my apartment before returning to a contented bachelor's life. Come the weekend, I would wake-up at my leisure (usually after whoring the night before), feed the cats and go to the gym, then on to breakfast on Castro Street with friends. There, over our meal, love and lust were discussed with an enthusiasm and relish normally reserved for idle gossip (which was never lacking at the table, either) and each of my past boyfriends was raked over the coals and my friends' true impressions of the men with whom I had fancied myself in love were finally revealed to me.

"I knew he wasn't for you from the beginning."

"I could tell he was psycho the moment I laid eyes on him."

"You're damn lucky this time."

I shrugged my shoulders.

Mick was (I now knew) prone to psychotic episodes that involved setting fires. This I learned when, after being unable to reach him at work or home for over a week, one of his roommates informed me that Mick had been kicked out of the apartment after starting a fire in his bedroom, a fire that the Fire Department deemed accidental despite the fact that it was lit beneath a chair in the middle of the floor. It was then that all the pieces fit together: The many allusions to the fire that had almost destroyed his childhood home, his habit of vanishing for a day or two at a time, his stories of vandalism at the Catholic high school where he spent so many hours inebriated on sacramental wine.

Thinking quickly, I asked the roommate to look for the set of keys Mick had to my apartment. They were still there on Mick's desk. Right after we'd spoken and the keys were found, Mick showed up at his old apartment asking for them and was told that I'd already collected them. Mick, thank goodness, was gone when I showed up on Rausch Street an hour later to fetch the keys that were tossed down to me from what had been Mick's bedroom window. After that day, I avoided Rausch Street, thanking what gods there were for delivering me safely from Mick.

"You need to be more careful."

"Next time could be the last time if you don't watch yourself."

"You know those red flags that jump out at you when you meet a guy like that? Guess what, Dave? They are *not* motioning you forward!"

I had to agree, of course, but this was neither the first nor the last time I would fall for a man that any sane, reasonable person would avoid. Oddly, though, after the initial fury at feeling betrayed, the requisite number of nights listening to suicidal music in a darkened apartment and crying my eyes out, and writing reams of bad poetry, I was neither bitter nor angry, only relieved to once again be back at the breakfast table on Castro Street with my friends.

"Next time, try dating someone normal."

"Someone you could take home to your parents."

"A guy who doesn't hold his knife and fork like a convict."

All of this was good advice, but we all knew that it wouldn't get me laid, or at least not with the kind of man who gave me the kind of intense, rough and tumble sex they all enjoyed hearing me talk about over our *après sport* meals. It was their advice, however well meant, that led me to Gavin: Charming, handsome, intelligent: Solipsistic, pathologically dishonest, shallow and narcissistic: All that and the sex was mediocre, too.

We met by accident, but he once said that he had seen me around the neighborhood, or going by on the Muni. He also said that he thought me very handsome, almost regal, with my new beard, which appealed to my considerable vanity. Our seeing each other, even meeting, though, was almost inevitable since he lived just across Market Street from me. He was shorter than me by a head, cute rather than handsome, and with a sparseness of body and facial hair that was oddly sexy on him, erupting here and there in dark and insistent clusters as if to bare witness to a barely sufficient production of testosterone. He was a little *zaftig* but muscular from time well spent at the gym, a decent kisser but hardly hung enough to compensate for his lack of technique or imagination.

At first he was charming, and I liked to be charmed.

He was also smart, having graduated from an Ivy League school, and this impressed me even if he wasn't clever in the way most of my friends were. He was well read but his opinions were the expected ones, as if regurgitated verbatim from *The New York Times* op/ed page; and while he kept current on the state of the world he never showed any particular insight into that crises we were currently living through: the Reagan Years.

I was also attracted to his snobbishness, sharing with him as I did a New England lineage considered ancient by American standards. Unlike me, however, he had never learned to discount it with the same breath he bragged about it, or to at least pay lip service to democracy. I found this refreshing at first, or would have, if his snobbery didn't eventually spill over into the kind racist and anti-Semitic slurs that denoted the ignorance of someone mired in his own mediocrity.

We didn't have sex (what he called Making Love) right away. We'd nod to each other on the street at first, maybe walk together and chat about nothing important, and flirt shamelessly. After several weeks of this, he invited me into his bed one Sunday afternoon in November and I had had to demur owing to a prior date. I attempted to instigate sex the next time I saw him a week or so later, but this time he declined – probably, I later realized, to maintain what he perceived to be a balance of power. When we finally did fuck, it was on his Murphy bed, on clean white sheets that I remember being in sparkling contrast to his otherwise dingy apartment.

Like me, he lived in a large, studio apartment built between the wars when the neighborhood (once called Uptown, but by the time we lived there known generically as Upper Market) was being developed. My studio, though, felt palatial in comparison. I was on the fourth floor, with a view of Mint Hill, in a building kept clean within and without. His second floor flat was in a building bordering on derelict and noisy every minute of the day due to the constant traffic outside his window.

Other than that we had sex that day, I remember little else. I recall that his mother phoned him right after we were finished and I saw at once that his relationship to her was a hostile one – always a red flag. If he hadn't been so damn cute I would probably have cut my losses and avoided him after that, but I was still young enough to be dissuaded from common sense by desire. Besides, he was clearly smitten with me and I didn't want to be dateless during the upcoming holidays.

This was his first Christmas in the City, my excuse to invite him to join me at a friend's home for Christmas dinner. He accepted and we walked together, but only after he had a visit to the emergency room for an impacted wisdom tooth; there he was given enough codeine to get him through the holiday weekend and sent on his way.

Sex was discussed over Christmas dinner, as might be expected of half a dozen gay men in their twenties. I watched Gavin blanch at some of the things discussed so casually (like one man's fetish for shaved genitalia) and thought his prudishness as charming as it was amusing, and something he would soon get over. It never occurred to me not to participate wholeheartedly in the conversation, or to not talk about the many men who had been in my life before him. If anything, I expected Gavin to join in and tell us about his past exploits. Our host, after all, was a former trick of mine turned buddy, a guy with whom I went trolling for men in sex clubs. This was our normal kind of discourse.

Gavin and I walked home together from Noe Valley rather than wait for the Muni. When we got to our corner of Market Street, Laguna Street and my apartment to the left, Guerrero Street and his apartment to the right, he said his tooth was hurting and that he would be going home alone. Disappointed but hardly put out, I kissed him goodnight and went home to change into something sleazy before heading back out. That night I met a man who became a regular fuck buddy, a man who fucked like a rabbit while talking a line of filth that left me hornier than when we had started. I said nothing about this to Gavin then, nor did I see any need to tell him. I assumed that, like me, he was seeing other guys.

The next weekend was New Years Eve and we had a date. This was the central reason why I kept dating him even after the red flags were flying: I wanted someone to kiss at midnight. We went out that night, danced for hours, got confetti in our hair, kissed as the clock struck twelve, and walked back to my place. He spent the night. We made love. Again, I don't remember much about the sex, and in fact I rarely commented on it in my diary, so it must have been unexceptional. I do remember waking up with him and being very happy. It was a beautiful clear morning, I recall, and I made us breakfast while we listened to Ella Fitzgerald.

That night, when I pulled back the covers as I got into bed, I found confetti on the sheets, and could even smell Gavin on the pillow. This felt very sweet and very romantic, and I enjoyed feeling nested in the bed we had fucked in the night before. The cat and I curled up together and I drifted off thinking how nice it might be settle down with someone as decent as Gavin.

1 January 1982

> *Gavin spent the night. We both slept well and with the cat (who seems to like him.) It was the best New Year's ever, partly because I had someone nice to share it with. While we were eating breakfast in my kitchen this morning, Gavin looked out the window and said: "Isn't this wonderful! A marvelous breakfast, a view of a Mission Style building with palm trees in the background, Ella's on the stereo, you're here! To think that Back East they recommend Valium." I might be falling.*

Even now, one can see why.
"That's so sweet," a friend said when I shared how I had felt.
"And he's such a nice boy," confirmed another friend. "For once."
"And cute."
"This one you could take home to meet your parents."
All this was true, but it was only a minor crush, more romantic than erotic, and so of less interest to me in the long term. Not that I didn't want to be in love with him. I felt myself falling in love (a very easy accomplishment for me at the time) but was waiting for the signal that would send me over Niagra Falls in a barrel.

We saw each other every weekend after that, sometimes meeting, for a meal or a movie, midweek as well. As I got to know him better, though, I became less interested in him. His snobbery was tiresome and affected – even by my standards. As he became more comfortable with me, his prejudices came to the fore, shocking me with their vulgarity. If my birthday weren't so soon, and if I so desperately didn't want to be dateless on my birthday, I would've stopped returning his calls sooner.

Despite all this dating, however, I think we only had sex a few more times. The last time was on my birthday after he took me out to dinner. I remember not being very enthusiastic at the time, but thought that it was the least I could do after such a nice dinner. One of the few details I can remember from sex with him was that he fucked me that night with only spit for lube, acting as if this were a pain-inducing punishment in payment for my past promiscuity. I played the part, winced and cried out at the appropriate moments, but was in reality unimpressed: His dick, while very hard, was on the small side of average, and hardly the punishing kind.

He often talked of the many friends he had made in San Francisco, nameless and faceless people I only heard about in passing: He went to concerts with them, ate in their homes, attended their parties. Initially, I looked forward to meeting them, to being his date at some social function or other, the invitations to which never came during the whole time we kept company.

He occasionally mentioned other men he had dated, but only derisively – like the boy who clapped between movements at the symphony. Neither I nor our common acquaintances ever saw Gavin at the symphony the entire time we knew him – which is not to say that he couldn't of, or that his story might not be true. Later I suspected that Gavin was the boy who clapped between movements while on a date with someone older and more sophisticated. Living in a privately defined universe as he did, I came to believe that Gavin projected the *faux pas* onto another boy, a boy without a name or history or description, to ease his own embarrassment.

It was around this time that his college buddy Fred – the only friend of Gavin's that I would ever meet – moved to San Francisco and into Gavin's small apartment.

"We're just friends," Gavin assured me – as if I had any investment in their sleeping arrangements, my little crush on him waning faster with each date.

As I got to know him better, I liked him less, and boredom soon replaced any romantic inclination I once held in his regard. I was still playing the field as before, unhindered. He called me one Thursday evening, just as I was heading out to the Jaguar for a fast fuck – or four.

"I was just on my way out."

"Really? Where?"

"Out."

"Oh, yes, I forgot. In California people have private lives."

I didn't think of this as deceptive. I just thought I was being discrete for once in my life.

A Nice Boy from a Good Family

As now seems inevitable, my friend James, who lived in my building on Laguna Street, met Fred, a fellow actor, by chance on the Muni – and they started dating. So now, with two supposed couples, there were double dates, dates that ended with a superficial kiss for me and Gavin, and all out coupling for James and Fred.

It quickly became clear to everyone that Gavin was in love with Fred, and had been since college. Fred, aware of this, spent less and less time at Gavin's flat, and more and more time with James in his little apartment. Eventually, Fred, unable to afford a place of his own with the salary he earned working at a record store on Castro Street (where he gave me ludicrously generous discounts whenever I shopped there), and unable to live peacefully with Gavin, went back home to his homophobic mother back east. James was saddened at Fred's departure, but soon got over it since he had (as was the custom in San Francisco at the time) been dating other men the entire time he had been dating Fred.

"You're not a slut if you have time to change the sheets," James liked to quip.

To which I could only respond: "Sheets?"

It ended completely for me when we went to see a new Truffaut film. All the way to the theatre he told me how he and Fred might be leaving San Francisco soon, perhaps to London or Paris, perhaps to New York, it all depending on numerous complicated dependencies. I thought (even hoped) at the time that his story might be true, but later I saw that it was just another tale told to impress me, or perhaps to make me jealous, or maybe just to convince his own sad soul that he and Fred had some kind of future together. To add to my annoyance that evening, Gavin, rather predictably I thought, loved the movie which I dismissed as excessively French, sensationalistic, and stupid to the point of insulting. I was so annoyed by the film and his praise for it that I could barely talk to Gavin on the bus ride home. When we parted company at our corner, I said goodnight without bothering to stop for the perfunctory goodnight kiss.

He called me the next day, Sunday, obviously casting his net out to bring me back into his bed. I was short and curt, excused myself saying I had plans to meet a friend, and left my apartment for an hour or two so as not to be made a complete liar of should he stoop so low as to walk by and see my light on, and me reading by it, from the street. I went home and wrote in my diary:

5 February 1982

Gavin: He is really not the sort of person I care to know.

A few mornings later (while staying home sick with the flu and running a low grade fever) I saw him at the local Safeway where I'd gone for a few necessities. I merely nodded to him and kept walking. He called me that afternoon to tell me was he hurt by the snub. I said I wasn't feeling well, which was true enough, but didn't apologize for the slight.

He didn't call me again after that.

I thought I had a new boyfriend in the works by then, anyway. I assumed Gavin had seen us around the neighborhood and retreated to his lair to lick his wounds. Thankfully, he never knew that come Valentines Day I was once again as dateless as I had always been on that day dedicated to romance.

The following fall, and several boyfriends later, on what would be my last trip to the Clap Clinic for almost two-decades, I learned that I had syphilis. Since it had been a while between visits to the clinic and I had had no symptoms for syphilis, I felt compelled, like the good citizen I am, to call everyone I could get a hold of that I might have infected, including Gavin.

17 December 1982

Conversation with Gavin Tuesday night. My excuse for calling was syphilis. I woke him as he works nights now. I hadn't remembered that we were dating a year ago when I called, but we know what Freud would say about that.

"David, I'm glad you called. I've been thinking a lot about you lately. I feel a lot is unresolved between us."

I let that slide and explained about catching syphilis, but he said he'd been tested since we'd last had sex. Which I think was a slight. Then again, he said that he felt "unresolved."

"You lost interest in me, Gav, and didn't have the guts to say it. We'd stopped having sex."

"No, that wasn't it at all. I felt hurt. I'd been objectified by you."

I admitted that that might be true and sort of apologized, but not really. Then came the clincher:

"*I loved you.*"

I'd've torn out his jugular vein if he said that to my face. Liar! Then he spoke of the fond memories he had of me, of our holiday season together last year, of how he refers to our liaison as his "Ella Fitzgerald Affair." Wanting to strike back, I told him how on Christmas day I left him at his place and went out and got royally fucked. He was as offended as I hoped he would be.

"*I was withholding sex to test faithfulness. I always do that.*"

"*Gav, that's manipulative and sick.*"

"*Of course it is. It's my way of creating what I need.*"

"*You act like a heterosexual woman.*"

Gavin then went on to tell me that Fred hadn't liked me, and that later he [Gavin] forbade James and Fred to mention me because it hurt him so much. I hung up and immediately called James who assured me that Fred did like me well enough, but that he was so furious with Gav that he hardly even said goodbye to him when he left for NYC. James also added that he never saw Gav except when I was around. Another fucking pathological liar. I should've seen it before this.

It was only in hind sight, of course, that it all became clear: His talk of "friends" that I never met or even saw him with, his many pretensions (like claiming to own a dinner jacket that he had no place to wear), his vague allusions to past boyfriends that remained mysteriously unformed in one's imagination, his many photos of himself but none of the friends and former lovers he was supposedly in constant touch with, his talk of parties or concerts attended with people whose paths never seemed to cross ours while we were out together in a very small city. Yes, it was possible that we might never run into other people he knew in town, but certainly if he had cared for me as he now said he had, I should have met them by plan if not by chance. He had met my friends, why had I not met his if all that he said was true? No doubt these were the same friends who had since our break-up set him up with his new boyfriend – something he was compelled to share with me between feeling unresolved and proclaiming his lost love for me.

It was hard to imagine anyone as cleverly passive aggressive, as versed in insinuated covert hostility as this handsome young man from whose embrace I had so fortunately escaped. Good riddance, I thought.

After this I never gave him more than the curtest nod when I saw him on the street. My friends, as always, concurred with my diagnosis, and joined me in snubbing him. When one is as young as I was then, one wants to be dramatic and being civil to Gavin would've cost me too many self-satisfied moments of feeling morally vindicated, if not morbidly self-righteous. I regret now being rude to him, but not my decision to have nothing more to do with him.

Several years later and well into the epidemic, happily partnered and with hardly a thought about Gavin or those ridiculous few months that were our affair, Dan, a mutual friend of Gavin's, James' and mine, told me that he had just seen Gavin, with his new boyfriend, in Provincetown. Dan and I were in the shower at the gym at the time, an odd yet perfectly natural place to share this kind of information. James had been dead a year or so and we were all feeling fragile, if not fearful, at the rapidly accumulating loss of so many friends now hanging heavy in our hearts. In that climate, hearing that someone was alive, but living elsewhere, was normally considered good news.

"Good for him," I managed to say, though to tell the truth I had thought Gavin might be dead since Mick and the two boyfriends who followed Gavin were dead or sick by this time. "So he moved back east?"

"Yeah. He seems happy, too," said Dan. "He said to say hello to you."

"Really?"

"Yeah. You know it was really hard on him when you guys broke up."

Still the liar, still the manipulator, I thought. Still trying to get a jab at me from across the country.

"Broke up?" I asked aloud, perhaps sounding more aghast than I really was at Gavin's claim on what had only been an apparent proximity. "I didn't know that we were ever together. It was nice of him to tell you about it."

But to myself I had to admit that sometimes we have only ourselves to blame.

An Amsterdam Night

*The only hope of our ever getting a really beautiful and vigorous
and charming civilization is to allow the whole world to fuck
and bugger and abuse themselves in public
and generally misbehave to their hearts' content.
– Lytton Strachey*

The Amsterdam Eagle, like the Argos just across the notorious Warmoesstraat, is all anyone could expect it to be: A maze of back rooms, cages, toilets and booths filled with the smell of sex, the grunting of men coupling in plain sight or behind locked doors, and the occasional "smack!" of flesh hitting flesh followed by the ever grateful groan. Urgent whispers in half a dozen languages filled my ears, broken by the barked commands, hungry pleas, and grateful sighs I'd understand in any language.

I'd returned to Amsterdam hoping it was as wonderful as I'd remembered, and afraid I might be disappointed since no reality could possibly live up to my memories of this sacred place. Anxious to relive the joy and spontaneity of sex between strangers that had disappeared in the States, I was back in this pocket of civilization I had come to think of as my second home, a city and country invincible to the Puritan backlash that had swept the North America, the UK and much of Europe during the 1980s.

Not much of a drinker, I bought a Coke and made my way to the back of the bar and waited. It was only eleven o'clock or so, early even for

An Amsterdam Night

a Thursday evening – the first night of the weekly long-weekend Amsterdam promotes to the tourists from Britain and Europe that flock here looking for the party they'd never find at home. Most won't go home until Sunday evening, others not until Monday night or even Tuesday morning, all of them wanting to make the most of their short holiday.

I lit a small cigar and watched the parade of men increase to droves as midnight drew nearer. They were North American, Spanish, Turkish, Scandinavian, Israeli, and who knew what else. Finally, I put out my cigar, finished the last swallow of my Coke and let my dick lead me to where it most wanted to go, deeper into the back of the narrow bar, further into the recesses of half-lit rooms and narrow stairways where the smell and sound of man-sex was as thick as a San Francisco fog. My cock tugged at my heart and I followed.

I saw him leaning against a post almost immediately. We glanced at each other, each liking what we saw. Both of us were bearded, muscular men around six feet tall, though he lacked the love handles that have followed me from birth. I wondered what he was in the mood for, top or bottom, and then wondered the same thing about myself as I went deeper into the darkness, admiring what I saw, excited by what I heard and wanting to be a part of it. I made a loop back and he was still there. We looked at each other again, the spark of mutual desire lighting the air as our eyes met.

I approached.

He nodded.

We kissed.

Our tongues met at the same moment our lips did, each of us exploring the other's mouth, hoping to find the deepest part of ourselves in the kiss, each of us looking for the special magic button that would send the other over the edge. I lost myself in the kiss. Our mouths stayed locked for long minutes, separating to catch our breath only to rejoin again. His hands ran over my body, pushing aside my leather jacket to pull on my nipples, undoing my Levis to grab my buttocks with both hands, pulling me closer to him.

He wore sweatpants and no underwear. I could feel his magnificent cock poking through the worn jersey as I caressed it with my hand. It was large and thick, typical of Dutch men, uncut but immaculately clean as is their wont. I had to have it.

I knelt, inhaling as much of his tool as I could, trying hard not to choke on so beautiful an organ. His hips moved back and forth as his cock tried to find the back of my throat. I swallowed all I could of it, felt the head expand in my esophagus and quickly backed off of it before I passed out.

A Nice Boy from a Good Family

When I stood up, he pulled me to him again, kissing me as he had before, swallowing all of me in his kiss as each hand grabbed an ass cheek and pulled them apart. I let my Levis drop to my knees and pulling back the foreskin slick with my spit, slipped his cock between my legs. It moved between my thighs as we kissed, thrusting between them, just beneath the hole it was searching for and wanting. I felt a finger enter my fuck hole. I let out a soft groan as his tongue moved further down my throat and his free hand pulled me even closer to him. Then a hand slapped my ass.

He'd found the trick to send me over the edge. I was in heaven. I was his.

Suddenly, he pulled away from a moment, caught his breath.

"Shall we have a drink?" he asked in perfect and beautifully accented English.

I almost laughed but didn't.

"Yeah," I answered at last, catching my breath again. "That would be great."

This is one of the amusing idiosyncrasies common to the Dutch. It didn't matter that we were on the verge of fucking, good manners called for a social exchange of some kind. We should at least know each other's names before we did it.

"What would you like?" he asked.

"*Spa Root*," I returned, asking for the local equivalent of a Calistoga.

He looked at me a moment with a surprised smile.

"You learn quickly."

"I try."

He ordered himself *een pilsje* and my *Spa Root*.

"*Dank u*," I said hoping to dazzle him with one of my few Dutch phrases.

He handed me my drink and we clinked bottles.

"*Proost!*"

"I'm Huib."

"Dave."

"Where are you from?"

"San Francisco."

"Ah! We got a lot of men from San Francisco here."

"I'm not surprised."

He nodded.

"You know a little *Nederland*, I see."

"Just enough to be polite."

"That's very sweet of you," he said putting his free hand on my ass again and pulling me a little closer. "But unnecessary."

His mouth reached out for mine and I was lost to the world again. I felt his cock harden again through the fabric of his sweats and my own worn Levis. His hand moved itself to the crack of my ass, caressing the seam that formed the crevice in my jeans.

A moment later we were apart again, panting, staring at each other.

"What shall we do about this?" he asked with another swallow of his beer."

An odd turn of phrase, I thought. I wondered if he'd learned it from a Brit he'd picked up sometime. It sounded like something a Brit would say. Or maybe it was Dutch colloquialism that sounded odd (but charming) to an American ear. In any case, it seemed pretty obvious what we both wanted. Did he want me to draw him a picture?

I nodded back towards the backroom we'd just come from.

He smiled.

A moment later we were behind a locked door. I was on my knees applying the condom, lubing it, stroking it, getting it ready for my hole. When I stood up again, Huib lubed my ass for me, stretching it open in preparation for the fat piece of meat he was going to shove inside me.

"Take it easy at first," I whispered. "I haven't had anything that big up my ass in a long time."

I saw that smirk again, this time the self-satisfied smile of a well-hung man who has once again been assured of his exceptional prowess. I leaned over, my back to him, smiling to myself and knowing I'd inadvertently added the aphrodisiac of a well stroked ego to the picture.

Then I felt him enter me. I winced, put my hand out to signal him to pause a moment. He did. Then, like the expert he clearly was, he pushed in further as he felt my fuck hole relax, pushing steadily in until all nine fucking inches were inside my ass. I groaned with delight, threw my head back and yelled out one of the first Dutch phrases I'd ever learned:

"*Neuk me!*"

Huib took me at my word and went to town.

Now we were making the noise, the grunting, the groaning, the slapping, the sweet and guttural Dutch obscenities that streamed out of Huib's mouth like water. My own sexual vocabulary, in Dutch anyway, limited to that one single cry was repeated again and again as I grabbed the walls to keep from being knocked against them. I felt as well as heard the wooden cabin creak and rock around us as I held myself steady against Huib's brilliant assault.

His cock pushed, pulled and pounded against my insides, punishing my prostate to a level of passion I'd not felt with a stranger in years. His hand slapped against my ass again and again as he grunted his pleasure, his joy, his satisfaction in my willingness to be his hole. I was the lucky boy who was the place he put his fat man meat tonight, happy to be the one he wanted, the one he fucked and filled with his ball juice. I grunted and groaned my own satisfaction in return, hoping the whole world heard us, that everyone in Amsterdam knew that tonight I was this hot man's fuck hole.

Then, after holding off I don't know how long, he grabbed my waist and raped my ass with renewed fury. I whacked at my own cock with an equal intensity, screaming for him to cum, to shoot it so deep inside me I could taste it. Then there was final blow to my ass, one last thrust as he growled his last growl, grunted his last coarse phrase, and collapsed on top of me. I felt his cock expand, contract, shoot, explode inside me as I shot my own load at the same time, shooting it against the wall of the little cabin four or five times. I almost collapsed to the floor, but managed to lean against the wall and support both our weights.

I heard Huib catching his breath, felt the sweat pour off his face and chest and down my back until it reached the crack of my ass. Then he regained himself, pulled himself up and slowly pulled his beautiful uncut cock out of me. There was an audible "plop" as I felt its absence, felt it leave where I knew it belonged.

I turned around and watched as he peeled off the condom, holding it up a moment so I could see the little cum-filled sack, the sight of which would always be a part of my sexual satisfaction, another erotic image to store away and remember in the years to come. Then we kissed, long and deep for several minutes more. For a moment I wished I were in my hotel room, in bed and ready to fall asleep with his man next to me, a man I was certain would be up and ready to fuck me again the first thing next morning. Then I remembered myself.

He smiled. I smiled.

"Another beer?" I offered, not wanting to let go of him just yet, but knowing I must since my own husband was out there on Warmoesstraat somewhere, possibly looking for me at that very moment. And if Huib and I ran into him there in the bar, I also knew that Huib, being Dutch, would handle it with great aplomb and courtesy, ending the evening by kissing us both goodnight and agreeing to meet us for dinner later in the week. He would (and did) do all this because he was a civilized man from a civilized country living in a civilized city – as well as man that, if circumstances had been different, I might have loved.

Mein Yiddishe Tate

Those for whom his tongue was no riddle were specters.
— Cynthia Ozick

Daddy fixations were a dirty little secret.

They smacked more of patriarchy (for obvious reasons) then other kinds of kinky sex, and were (like all forms of kink) politically suspect. Even more politically dangerous was the flirtatious fulfillment of Freudian theory: If I was looking for a Father Figure, then I must be emotionally immature after all, like Freud said, and am only compounding the neurosis when I called my lover 'Daddy.' Or so some outsiders would have had us believe. But when a man I was dating wanted me to call him Daddy as well as Master, to control me as fathers do their sons rather than as a Master controls his slaves, I was hooked like a fish on a line by the sheer perversity of the scene. I could still be tied up, humiliated and made to service my Master's friends as before, only now I called him 'Daddy' letting the soubriquet be savored by all who heard it.

When I found myself in another man's bed a year later, bound and naked as I watched him put on his pajamas after fucking and flogging me, I thanked him for disciplining and using me so well.

"My pleasure, boy. Daddy had fun tonight, too."

I smiled, pleased that I had pleased him.

He got into bed, spreading the covers over us as he circled me in his big, muscular arms.

"If you keep our private little games a secret," he whispered into my ear as he held me close, "you and Daddy can play them *forever*."

I sighed deeply at these words. My cock was suddenly very hard again, but being bound I couldn't touch it. Instead I snuggled deeply into his broad, hairy chest and inhaled his scent.

"Yes, Daddy," I murmured into the darkness. "I can keep a secret."

"That's my good boy."

This, I thought, is as good as it gets. I'm home.

I hadn't counted on meeting David Lourea.

When we met at the Catacombs he was in full leather and I was naked. He was handsomer than any man I'd seen before: a *Yiddishe punim* with wavy black hair, huge brown eyes, a brilliant smile, a thick black mustache, an olive complexion, and high Semitic cheekbones. I wanted him bad. And I got him bad.

Perhaps, on introducing ourselves, we were both a little put off at being with another man named David. I know I was; but since I wasn't looking to stand beneath the *chuppah* when I approached him, I didn't let it bother me. At that moment, I was just looking to get done by a very hot man in front of the crowd gathered at the Catacombs.

We made small talk and I casually mentioned that I liked his boots, and that I would like to lick them and to be his slave – if only for that night. He nodded and said, "Maybe later." For some reason I wasn't put off by this. Even while I watched him play with a friend of mine, a beautiful boy who just had recently posed for Colt Studio (his life-long ambition up to that time) I waited patiently, certain that my turn would come. It did, and later I wrote all about it (with my usual enthusiasm) in my diary.

I also knew from the start that this would be an important conquest and that a good report from him would assure my being invited back to the Catacombs. Later on I discovered that he was bisexual, with a wife and a male lover. I found this information titillating, and enjoyed telling all my friends that I'd done a married man. David and I would run into each other now and then after that, play at the Catacombs occasionally, but I never let my heart get involved with him despite his many charms. As much of a crush as I had on him, I still wanted no part of the complex web of relationships that David and his bisexual wife were professed to have. While hardly a sexual conservative, and certainly not monogamous, I thought this sort of "civilized" openness somewhat dated by, what was then, the early 1980s.

"I don't want to date him seriously under the current circumstances," I told our mutual friend, Cynthia Slater, after she told me that David had a new boyfriend. "But it would still be nice to be asked."

A few years later – quite suddenly it seems to me now, but maybe not since I was by then approaching 30 – I decided that I was bored with dating an assortment of men and that I wanted to "settle down." Just as suddenly, the pool of prospective partners I was willing to consider as husband material consisted almost exclusively of Jewish men.

It was right after an intense but short love affair had ended that I ran into David at *schule*. I knew my most recent ex-boyfriend would be going to San Francisco's other queer synagogue, so I went to this one that night for no reason other than to worship, a pleasure I'd only just discovered thanks to this same ex-boyfriend (Jason Gaber, may he rest in peace) to whom I am now eternally grateful.

"Are you here with you're boyfriend?" David asked.

"No, Jason and I broke up," I answered as casually as I could. I knew already that David and his wife were getting divorced. I had expressed no joy at this news when I'd heard it a few months before, but had secretly hoped ever since that we might eventually get together.

His face lit up. "Well maybe after services we can...?"

"Not tonight," I answered truthfully. "I have a blind date. How about next week?"

"Sure," he answered. "I'll look forward to it."

I knew that I was already falling in love with him but held my emotions in check. I remembered something Andrew Holleran had written about falling in love being like cooking a pot roast and hence all a matter of timing: For the first time in my life, I played it cool. I would let him call me first. And he did, a few nights later.

As much as I looked forward to seeing David, and to having a real date with him, I did not expect to forge any new ground when it came to sex. I was sure I had done it all. Whatever we did sexually, be it kinky or vanilla, it would be sure to be fun sex – just nothing to send new shivers down my spine as my cock unexpectedly hardened anew, dripping sudden expectation. But again, I underestimated David Lourea.

Quite naturally, it seemed, we fell into a Daddy-boy scene. I was spanked for being a bad boy and jerking-off in the men's room at work, then fucked long and hard as only he could fuck. His cock was only average, but he had a great technique that had me squirming under him, wanting more and more of him as he did his level best to give it all to me.

When he'd finished fucking me, he rolled me over in his arms and held me while I wanked-off. One hand's fingers played with my prostate while the other pulled on my nipples. Then I heard the words that defined us as the couple we would become, the added kink that had heretofore gone untapped.

"*Sheyna boychick.*"

All the time I was jerking-off, he murmured to me in Yiddish: I was his *sheyna boychick*; I was as pretty as the moon; I was my *tate's* darling. Suddenly *Mamma Loshn* felt like a forbidden tongue, the language of our most perverse desires. My cock was rock hard. I cried out as I shot my load over our shoulders where it hit the headboard behind us several times in rapid succession.

"*Tate!* I'm cumming, *Tate*, I'm cumming!"

"That's a good *tatela*. Make *Tate* proud..."

The rest of that night, being held tight against his hairy body as we slept, I felt dirty and excited at the same time. It was as if we'd done something blasphemous – only it was something we could feel good about because it only *felt* forbidden.

We rarely spoke about our new language of desire, however, even between ourselves. It was our secret, and one we hardly dare mention even when we were alone together. We only spoke it when we fucked.

What I did not know until then was that Yiddish was his first language. Raised by his grandmother until he was five years old, Yiddish was all he spoke until he was sent to kindergarten where he learned English on his own. While roughly the same age as my eldest brother, he was still my *Yiddishe Tate*, the embodiment of an implied but fictional incest that became the finest expression of what would be our love.

Any boy honest enough to tell you about belonging to his Daddy will also tell you that part of the appeal of being a boy is, after all, how dirty it lets him feel. It is the naughty secret that becomes the sudden bemused smile coming out of nowhere the next day on the job, or sitting on the streetcar home, or between sets of bench presses at the gym.

Was I in love, friends asked, or just well fucked? I couldn't tell them at first for fear of spoiling something so precious that it defied all language but it's own perverse code. Eventually everyone knew about us. We were an established couple before long, known to be kinky and with a reputation far wilder than anything we ever lived up to in our real lives.

We often played publicly over the years, mostly because I enjoyed it so much. We played either at different SM clubs, or at the leather bars along Folsom Street, or at friends' private parties where we were always expected to give some kind of performance. At these times I called him Sir, Master, or Daddy as I knelt at his booted feet on the end of a leash. Only in private did *Mamma Loshn* become *Tate Loshn*, the words we etched into each other's hearts.

Eight years later, while he lay dying, it was in the broken Yiddish phrases that he had taught me that I tried to express my love for him, hoping *Mamma Loshn* would penetrate the coma where mere English could not.

Two Weddings, One *Tuchas:*
An Unfortunate, But Mostly True, Love Story

*And what writer could deny that, even in moments
of real affliction, he is always accompanied by an imp taking notes?*
– Sir Harold Nicholson

The first advice ever given to me by an editor[25] (and of a gay skin magazine, no less) was the expected, "Continue to write what you know." To which was added, rather unexpectedly, "And, if at all possible, tell the truth." It is the later, of course, that is the greatest challenge.

This much at least is true: The other three principles in this tale are all dead and I can use their names without prejudice.

It's 1990 and I'm at Blow Buddies, one of the first sex clubs to re-emerge after the dearth of gay male sex venues that had been the bane of San Francisco since 1984. I see him and there is an instant energy, the spark of mutual lust, as our eyes meet. He isn't even my type. I usually lean towards hairy Mediterranean men with dark skin and black hair, brilliant smiles, and

---

25 Steven Saylor at *Drummer*.

flashing brown eyes; men close to me in height; men who spend at least as much time at the gym as I do. Rick is fair-haired and blue-eyed, has a gap between his front teeth that is oddly sexy, is a full head shorter than me, and has an average body with almost no body hair between his pubes and perfect blonde beard. But, oh, yeah, he has a big cock.[26]

We kiss for a very long time, sucking each other's dicks and nipples. And, since fucking, even with condoms, is against club rules, I keep putting his fat cock between my thighs to get the feel of the girth of his dick between my legs, imagining what it would be like to be fucked by him. Eventually we part company, neither of us having cum, and I ask him if he has a lover though I already know the answer.

"Yeah," he answers with a bashful look to the floor, embarrassed to be caught outside the nest.

"Thought so. Me too."

"Yeah?"

"Yeah. Let's get together sometime and try this laying down."

"Yeah, lets."[27]

But we don't. Not yet.

My husband, David, and I had never been monogamous. Since he worked odd hours as a therapist, and we didn't get to spend as much time together as we wanted, I confined my philandering to those times we couldn't be together, or when he was too tired to go out when I wanted to play. My pattern with tricks was (and is) to lose interest in them after fucking two or three times. David's pattern was to become friends with his playmates,

---

26 Years later he asked if I remembered what I wore that night.
"Tight jeans?"
"Army fatigues. Torn-up army fatigues tucked into your boots that dropped around your ankles when you undid them."
"You remember?"
"It was so damn sexy, Dave. How could I forget?"
Typical of my vanity, I remember the conversation better than the details of that night.

27 Again, years later, Rick told me that he hadn't even been heading to Blow Buddies that night. He'd been driving down Folsom Street when he saw a hot man in black leather chaps go into the club. Until that moment he didn't know that there was anything in the unmarked building. A few minutes later he was at the same door, pursuing the man in black leather chaps but finding me.

sometimes inadvertently encouraging them to fall in love with him.[28] Rick (for that was his name) was different from my other tricks from the very beginning, and something deep in my gut told me to give him a wide berth, to avoid the inevitable collision as long as I could.

Maybe it was the Seven Year Itch. Maybe I missed the rush of being newly in love. Maybe I missed the early days of my relationship with David when we couldn't get enough of each other. Maybe I was sick of death and thought Rick's attention would be the balm to heal a heart repeatedly broken by the loss of friends. Maybe I was just bored. Whatever the reasons (and there are no good ones) I dismissed the inner warnings and waited for the day when Rick and I would finally fuck.

A new, unlicensed sex club has emerged a few doors down from The Power House on Folsom Street. Called The Night Gallery[29], it's notoriously sleazy in all the right ways. It's there where I finally run into Rick again. As soon as our eyes meet the electric spark flashes between us. We kiss. This time we're all over each other: Lips lock; hands search for buttons and buckles to undo, his fat cock finally finds my asshole. I slip off my denim shorts[30] and lean back against the dirty old couch in the center of the room. My booted feet rest on his shoulders as his own Levi's are pushed down to his knees. I hand him the condom and lube after lubing my fuckhole. He puts it on deftly, obviously familiar with rubbers,[31] and enters me.

Or he tries to enter. I'm so out of practice with a dick of his size that I ask him to pull out and try again several times before I'm comfortable with the

---

28 When David died and I went through his desk, I found stacks of love letters, in addition to my own, sent to him by men and women who mistook his need for intimacy during casual sex with love. I shook my head in delight and dismay at these (perhaps) accidental conquests.

29 When one entered The Night Gallery one was greeted with, "Hey, thanks for coming to my party. I'm asking all my friends to chip in five dollars to help cover expenses." It went on for years, a well-known secret and the butt of numerous jokes.

30 Denim shorts, cut-off Levis with the hem folded-over an inch or two above the knee, was *de rigueur* ACT UP wear at the time, especially when worn, as I wore them, with calf-high Doc Marten's.

31 I eventually learned that his first sexual relationship had been with a girl in high school and that they routinely used condoms for sex, hence his comfort and ease with wearing them. Despite my years doing safe sex education in the 1980s, however, I was never completely comfortable wearing condoms or feeling them inside me.

whole girth and length of his cock. When I relax enough to enjoy it however, I'm shameless – writhing, screaming, and grabbing his head for more kisses. We attract a crowd, as might be expected, an aphrodisiac for both of us. We both hold off for as long as we can, me stroking my own cock, Rick pounding inside of me. We come together.

I've never had much invested in simultaneous orgasms before, but now, with Rick, it becomes my new gold standard for fucking

8 July 1991

I met this guy, Rick, and played with him a couple of times last year when I saw him at sex clubs. He has a lover who thinks they're monogamous. (Right!) We ran into each other at a sex party over the weekend and fucked with a vengeance. It was incredible. And the lust is so mutual. This time we exchanged our work phone numbers and talked about doing lunch sometime, and maybe getting together when one of our husbands is out of town. (His works a swing shift a lot.) I had jerked-off thinking about him several times since I'd seen him last, and now that I've had my way with him, I can't get him out of my mind. I know I'm not in love with him. But I want him. It's just desire, but desire can take me places where nothing else can. I'm contemplating asking if wants to have an affair. Nothing heavy. Just frequent, hot, steamy, nasty sex.

I've never felt this way before. I've had crushes but never pursued them further than a few tumbles in bed. This guy I want to stay around a while, to feel our bodies come together with a terrific crash and thunder. And I want lots of it. Until we get tired of it anyway. Or – let me be honest – until I get tired of him. In the mean time, I'm afraid to call him because I don't know what I'll do. Or what he'll do. Though he obviously is as turned on to me as I am to him. I mean, his kisses take me over the edge. What's love got to do with it? Nothing. What has desire got to do with it? Everything.

The only moral issue is, as I see it, his husband's belief (sure) that they're monogamous. But if Rick is lying to him, the relationship can't last, can it? If I don't do it, someone

else will. Of course, David's feelings have to be considered. But he doesn't think we're monogamous, so it's not quite the same. I suspect though, that as soon as we get down to constraints of time and place, we may be through with each other. That does happen to me a lot. Sex should be simpler than it is, but then the drama that surrounds it is part of what makes it so much fun.

We run into each other again – same time and place – a few weeks later. The same scene, the same hole filled, and once again we shoot our loads at the same time. Another crowd surrounds us, and as I wipe the copious cum from my chest and abdomen, I push away the wandering hands of the unwanted, saying:
"Show's over, guys."

We learned something valuable about each other at this juncture: Both our partners had AIDS, both were sick but still working, and both of us needed the distraction of the relationship we were now forging. This was our primary rationale for what was to come (and cum): Lust was the drug to keep us sane while the ones we loved died.

While we continued to use condoms, I hated them. I was (and am) sensitive to latex, which was the reason I hadn't been fucked in a while – not even by David. Only an exceptional dick like Rick's, and the promise of truly amazing sex, motivated me to use them and suffer the subsequent ongoing discomfort that followed each fuck for several days. This was another secret I kept from David: Someone else was fucking me while I was refusing him the same privilege. Aware of this, and feeling like a *schmuck*, I quickly, if only temporarily, remedied the situation with David. But only to assuage my guilt.[32]

---

[32] That I was only letting him fuck me out of guilt and not out of love did not cross my mind at a time when we were both shell-shocked from the constant bombardment of the deaths of friends. I want to believe that I wasn't the only one not thinking clearly during those desperate years, though this will never excuse my behavior, nor did it make it easier to forgive myself after David died.

22 July 2001

David may go to LA this weekend, and if he does, I'll call Rick. Oh, baby. I haven't spoken to him since I called him two weeks ago. I still want him. But only sexually. It will pass sooner or later, if I get to do it with him a few times. Nothing like experience to weaken desire. Maybe he'd not shave for a day or two if I asked him nicely? Then I could feel his stubble when we kissed. I've got to stop thinking about him.

Rick and I call each other at work now, make dates for sex but are circumspect in our relationship to each other, respecting the priority of each other's marriage. When David is out of town, I invite Rick over for a nice long fuck on our bed.

"How bad do you want to be?" I ask.

He looked at me as if I were about to challenge him.

"Sit on my face."

Rick has the sweetest little butt hole, pink and tight and delectable. I rim him for several minutes before he returns the favor. I wanted to ask him to put his cock in without the condom but don't dare. He fucks me as usual. We came together as usual.

9 September 1991

The first night David was gone, I saw Rick. He came over and we fucked like minks. He's incredible sexually. He's like me: Sleazy, noisy, rough and tumble, likes to talk trash. We fucked for hours, even though we both were only able to cum once, the first round taking it all out of us. We kept fucking anyway. His dick is perfect. It fits inside me like it belongs there, hits all the right places when he fucks me, pushes the cum right out of my balls. I can only recall two other men [Jan and Rich] who did to me what Rick does. And it's mutual. We were both so turned on, so excited by each other, we couldn't stop even when we really couldn't go on.

I asked him if he wanted, since we were both happily married, to have a sexual affair.

"I thought you'd never ask," he answered.

Don't know how or when, but we have to meet again. I even have this fantasy of running away to Mexico with him, to Zehuatenejo, for a week of non-stop fucking, just to get it out of my system. But maybe it wouldn't. Which would be dangerous.

I told him that his lover has to have a clue about his extra curricular activities, but he insists that the man is blind. I don't believe it. He'd have to be a fool. He just doesn't want to know – which is foolish. Especially with boys like me around. I'm so naughty, such a tramp. But it's all desire, lust and need. I like Rick and will probably like him more as I get to know him, but my motivating force is desire. And he's German! What's the world coming to? I'm hot to trot for a guy who's blonde and Aryan, and totally not my type at all! At least he's also hot to trot for me. There's nothing like mutual lust/desire/need. Unless, of course, you add love to the mix. But love isn't in the picture here and it had better stay away for our mutual well being. I'm not worried about that, though perhaps I should be.

When my friend Pete is in the hospital a month later, I have keys to his apartment to check mail and water plants. I take Rick there for sex.
"Since we've never actually discussed IT before, I need to ask –."
"Am I positive? Yeah. I always knew you were. I can taste the AZT sometimes when I kiss you."

Another night, he's driving me home from a sex party on 14th Street (David is out of town with our car); he asks if we aren't thinking the same thing about our relationship. I know what he's hinting at, but chose to be evasive, saying only that our relationship is clean, uncomplicated, and that I suspect we're traveling along parallel lines to the same conclusion.
I know this is a bullshit answer.
I also know that we're falling in love with each other.

22 January 1992

David and I had a very difficult time over the holidays. He even got crazy enough to want to break-up once. But we talked through it (imagine how easy that was for me!)[33], though, and we're still together – basically, I think, because we belong together.

During this awful time, David read my diary, which he rationalized by saying he needed to know what was going on inside me. And he read about Rick with the perfect dick. Which brought on another fight. I still resent the intrusion, the invasion of my privacy. But we also come from two very different cultural perspectives: His family is always expressing their feelings, while mine respects privacy and expects it to be respected. He knows what he did was wrong, and a violation, but doesn't understand how very painful it is for me to know that he has, in some (very bad) way, raped me. I don't like how it feels and I want to protect myself from other invasions. And to get back at him. Which I sort of did, by flogging him at a New Year's Eve party, to the disco version of the Hallelujah Chorus. We both enjoyed that.

But I hadn't told him about how good sex with Rick is because I didn't think he needed/wanted to know. I sure wouldn't want to know that he was having better sex with someone else than he ever had with me. And now, since he knows that Rick is part German, he refers to him as "that Nazi pig." Which has, I'm glad to say, become something of a joke.

What we didn't, and couldn't, know was that this would be David's last New Year's celebration.

---

33 While David was the product of Eastern European Jews, I'm descended from a dozen generations of New England Puritans. The difference between our families, and our ways of dealing (or not dealing) with our feelings, was like the famous dinner scene in Woody Allen's **Annie Hall**. David's family constantly emoted while mine was (and is) embarrassed by any open demonstration of strong feelings.

Pete, one of my best friends for ten years or so, is dead. I'm an emotional wreck for weeks as I call his family and friends, handle the details of his estate, and close up his apartment. My grief allows me more space, though, space I take advantage of to spend time with Rick. So I ask him out for dinner.

The meal is initially awkward but enjoyable. We never really talked for more than a few minutes before. Now we're forced (by our date) to actually converse. Conversation grows more relaxed the more we eat. When it's over, we kiss goodbye, deeply, fully, communicating our shared longing for each other.

After that we get together for coffee or dinner or a drink at least once a week. When a friend sees us together, I tell him that he didn't see me there with Rick, and much to my relief he agrees to the deception.

Still, the dirty-four-letter-word has been never spoken between us.

30 March 1992

> ***I've seen Rick a few more times. And it's always exciting/ fun. And uncomplicated. David asks me about him but I resist saying anything. Rick is a nice guy, and I'm glad that we're becoming friends as well as fuck buddies. He once said that he loved it when I came while he's fucking me with his fat dick.***
>
> ***"You like seeing me reduced to a bowl of jelly?" I asked.***
>
> ***He smiled.***
>
> ***"Well, yeah."***
>
> ***How could I not like a guy like that? Especially when he's safely married?***

No sooner do I settle Pete's estate than David is seriously ill. He is sadly apologetic for getting sick so soon after Pete has died, breaking my heart where I had thought there was nothing left to break. I take on the responsibility of his care, reduce my hours at work, set up needed home care, and enlist any and all assistance offered by our friends and family. Unasked for by me, David institutes my weekly night out. Friday or Saturday night, someone spends the evening with David and I go out to play. I almost always meet Rick on these excursions, but admit only to nameless strangers at Blow Buddies when David asks me if I had a good time.

13 April 1992

> *I saw Rick again this last weekend. He put a smile on my face as usual. We were at a play party, fucking up a storm, when this guy from my gym came by and watched us while grabbing his crotch with that come hither look in his eyes. He's very cute, but he's never given me the time of day before. Now I should have sex with him? Or maybe it was just Rick he wanted? No, I don't think so. It was the two of us and the hot time we were obviously having at the party. And we always get an audience when we fuck at parties. Anyway, I had to stop in the middle of it all to ask him about his T-cells to make sure cryptosporidium[34] wouldn't be an issue for him (though he would likely have been exposed the last few times we fucked if I'm carrying it). Hardly romantic or sexy, but all part of being a party boy in the 90s. He was cool about it, of course, and proceeded to fuck me raw.[35] What a guy.*

"I'm having an affair," I tell a friend, one my oldest and still surviving friends from my early years in San Francisco. We are driving to a party while David stays home, David not feeling well enough to go with us. "I've never had an affair before. David has but I haven't. I've only tricked before."

"Are you going to let it interfere with your relationship with David?"

"No."

"And you're not going abandon David now that he needs you more than ever?"

"Absolutely not!"

---

34 David had been diagnosed with *cryptosporidium* (the opportunistic infection that would eventually kill him) and there was some concern about me being exposed to it in my caring for him and spreading it to someone else. Whether or not *cryptosporidium* is a significant issue to one's health depends on the strength of one's immune system, hence I wanted to know Rick's CD4 count.

35 By which I meant, my fuckhole felt raw when it was over. Raw had not yet become a popular euphemism for unprotected sex.

"Then there isn't anything to discuss. This guy is clearly giving you something David can't give you right now."

This is not only what I want to hear, but probably true. More importantly, I'm absolved.

18 May 1992

I saw Rick on Saturday night. We met at Eros where we made a spectacle of ourselves not once but twice. Can't believe we did all we did. Fucked me cross-eyed. He even told me that he doesn't usually enjoy being the top as much as he does with me. Must be me, huh? Anyway, his lover, Steve, is not doing well but won't go on disability. He just works and sleeps. Rick fusses over him a lot but can't even get him to take it any easier. I didn't tell Rick this (I can see how worried he is about Steve), but I suspect that Steve is one of those men who needs to work. He may already know (consciously or unconsciously) that his illness will progress faster if he doesn't work. Fortunately that's not our problem. David can still see clients and thus keep as busy as he needs, or is able, to be.

"If David weren't one of the parties involved in this triad," my best friend, Mike, tells me around the same time, "and he were on the outside looking in, you know that he'd approve of it. As long as you put David first, that is."

Again, absolution.

A trip to Key West over Halloween weekend (with a group of gay friends I'd met through comic book fandom) had been in the planning for almost a year. Unable to go (or perhaps just not wanting to spend a weekend with a bunch of queer comic book fanatics), David insisted that I go without him. Taking advantage of the opportunity, I invited Rick to join me there. Once in Key West, I explained to my friends that David was dying, but not who Rick was. Only to my closest friend in the group did I confide that I was in love with Rick.

As soon as we're alone together, we're fucking.
"Put it in me."

"I'm not wearing a condom."
"I know. I want you without the condom."
Uncomfortable but eager, he complies with my request.
"I want you, David. I want you so much."
"You've got me Rick."
"Are you my baby? Are you my baby?"
"Yeah, I'm your baby."
"I **want** you, baby. I **need** you, baby."

There is a pause as he continues fucking me, a pause filled with words waiting to be said.

"You're going to make me say it first, aren't you? You son-of-a-bitch, you're going to make me say it first!"
"Say it, David! Say it!"

Another pause passes between us as he pounds his dick deep inside of me, as if fucking me would force the words from me.

"I love you!" *I finally scream.* "I love you!"

It's awful, that split second, that eternal blip on the cosmic counter, as I wait for his response. Then he smiles, as I've never seen him smile before.

"I love you," *he says.* "I love you, too!"

And we come together. He comes inside me and I revel in the knowledge that his seed is now a part of me forever. I am an incubus. I am in love.

After the weekend was over and we had said goodbye to the other guys, Rick and I drove up the Keys to Miami where I dropped him at the airport. Unable to book a flight home that day, I spent the night in Miami Beach. I was excited and miserable at the same time, ate too much dinner only to throw it up from nervousness, went for a long walk along the boardwalk where I met a lady feeding feral cats and gave her twenty dollars. I was in love. I was insane. My husband was dying and I already had a new one in the wings. I was happy, if miserable, in Rick's absence.

I called David that night and told him that I hated Miami, which was true.

I called Rick the next morning.

2 November 1992

>"Is this my baby?"

>"I'm glad you called. I've missed you."

>"Good. I miss you."

>"How's Miami?"

>"I hate it."

>"I love you."

>"I love you."

>"What've you been doing?"

>"Swam in the ocean, which was great. Fell asleep after a nice long walk on the boardwalk. Woke-up at five this morning."

>"You must have been a tired baby."

>"Yeah."

>"I'm so glad you called. I'm head over heals in love with you."

>"I love you, sweet baby."

Rick met me at the airport when I flew home that afternoon.

David was in the hospital. He went in and out of the hospital for the next ten days. Then he died.

David had asked me to sit *shiva*,[36] telling me I would need the comfort of being cared for by the community. I complied with his request out of respect for him, not knowing until it happened how right he was.

---

36 *Shiva* is the first seven days of mourning in the Jewish tradition. During these seven days the community has an obligation to feed and look after and listen to the mourner. During *shiva* the mourner may scream, cry, even curse G-d, and is under no obligation to consider anyone else's feeling. Completely opposite of the Unitarian (non) tradition that I grew-up with, it's a luxury every widow/er should have.

Rick made an appearance at *shiva*. My friends asked each other who he was. No one yet knew.

16 December 1992

Have I mentioned Rick's lover, Steve? Being the bright boy he is, Steve figured out that I existed. He even figured out who I was when a mutual friend (Steve and I have met exactly once) saw Rick and me together[37]. It probably had something to do with Rick spending the night with me.[38] Anyway, Steve and Rick keep talking it out and have come to some kind of arrangement where Rick stays with me twice a week (though never the same two nights because I don't want to be on a schedule, but generally Friday or Saturday and one school night) and the occasional weekend away. It seems to be working out okay. I don't even think I want to see more of him than that because I'm still grieving for David and dealing with the enormity of my loss. I'm afraid that spending too much time with him will keep me from feeling all I need to feel over David's loss. When I explained this to Rick, he was completely understanding and made it clear that he wanted me to tell him when I needed more time to myself or felt that we were rushing it. In this regard, he's a lot like David.

I should have listened to myself.

At some point Rick and Steve had a fight that resulted in Rick staying with me almost every night, even bringing his cat Teddie Bear to live with my three cats and two dogs. (His cat lived with me until her death 12 years later.) And I did become dependent on Rick. He was the drug that kept me from feeling the depth of my loss. During the next eight months we went to

---

37 I later learned that the mutual friend, knowing that some things are better not known, said nothing to Steve about seeing us together, thereby disproving my assumption that everyone is as indiscrete as me.

38 I often accused Rick of forcing the confrontation with Steve intentionally, which he denied. I later came to realize that Rick just wasn't that complex a person and avoided the kind of introspection and self-analysis that most of my friends and I indulge in on a daily basis.

Amsterdam with some women friends of mine, then later to Cabo San Lucas, and even Australia.

7 April 1992 (Amsterdam)

> *At one point, while Rick was taking a nap, I was writing in here and suddenly realized how much I missed David. I ran to Arlene[39] and Joy's room in tears. They comforted me, Arlene saying that David was happy with me, that he knew he could count on me and that I was there for him. I needed to hear this since I felt like a failure, like I'd betrayed him. Arlene pointed out that David had his stuff to deal with as much as I did, and that we had both made an effort to make the relationship work. I felt better, needing to hear this to let go of the sense of failure I've felt since David died.*

Slowly Rick came to the conclusion that he needed to return to Steve. This was the right thing for him to do, I knew. I wanted to believe (and still believe) that I would never have left David for Rick had our places been reversed, and certainly would have taken greater care not to hurt David than Rick had taken with Steve. So I couldn't fault Rick with his decision to return to Steve, neither ethically nor personally, as unhappy as it made me. I wish I could say that I rose to occasion, but I didn't. I was bitter, petty, and accusatory, doing my best to alienate Rick.

To make matters the worse, a cough Rick had developed during our trip to Australia was eventually diagnosed at *pneumocystis carinii* pneumonia. Rick got sick, was hospitalized, got better and went home. Then I got sick. Then Steve died. Then I got worse and almost died during a month long hospital stay.

When I eventually returned home, I was still resentful of Rick, still furious at what I considered his abandonment of me. After several months, though, after talking it over with friends (one of whom kindly pointed out to me that it's usually what we neglect to do rather than what we actually do, that we regret) I finally got bigger than myself (as David would have put it) and called Rick. He had Kaposi's *sarcoma* by this time, had lost most of his senses of taste and smell, and tired easily. We managed to maintain a sort of

---

39 A fellow South Philadelphia Jew, Arlene was David's best friend for a dozen or more years. Joy is one my best friends, and the mother of my daughter.

friendship after that, even having more of that sensational sex once in a while, though now he (wisely) insisted on the rubbers I hated. It was then I put into words what I had always known: Rick was never good at communicating except with fucking, and when I wasn't getting fucked by him I'd felt the void of his absence all the more acutely because he had no words to fill it with as David, or another almost any other lover, would.

I talked to my rabbi about this insight, expressing my gratitude that I could finally let go of the all the misdirected anger I'd felt towards Rick during those long miserable months. Now I was just grateful for the time I'd had with him even if I'd failed to handle to relationship with anything approaching the acquired wisdom of my years.

"You needed him and he was there for you for as long as he could. But there's an old Yiddish expression: You can't dance at two weddings with one *tuchas*. And that's what he tried to do. But couldn't. He had to make a choice, and he made the right one, painful as it was for you. I'm glad that you can see that now too."

Rick died in September of 1995, and I wept once more to lose someone I loved.

After he died, I hung Rick's picture on my wall (something I'd not done before) to remind myself that once I was very much in love with him, and he with me. We loved too well rather than wisely, but we did love.

I wish that I had some astute observation to make about love, about love's necessity, about how - in the end - it's only love that matters. That would be a fit ending for a story I never thought I'd have the *chutzpah* to tell; and having told it, I see now how rarely Love and Truth keep the same company, how even more rarely they share the same bed.

But how precious, how sweet is the honeyed Lethe of a new lover's kiss!

A Nice Boy from a Good Family

"And what should I do in Illyria?"
Notes of a Survivor

Which shall I follow,
And following die?
No longer count on me
But to say good-bye.
– Stevie Smith

    I have come to dislike the word "survivor". Like so many other perfectly good words that become casualties of changing fashions in language (e.g., est, mellow-speak, psycho-babble, recovery lingo, new age-isms), it has come to mean more and less than it ought. I know, for instance, that I started having safe sex in 1982, and am reasonably certain that I was infected with HIV before then, which makes me what is known as a long term survivor – a term wrought with contradictions.

    The very word "survivor" indicates that the epidemic is over, that I can now spend the rest of a normal life dealing with the loss and pain of the last 15 years. Yet we all know that the chances of my surviving the ravages of this pesky virus are, in the long run, nil short of a forthcoming medical miracle. Still, I continue to hope I will survive the epidemic, that I will have a few friends left when it is over to talk about the days before the plague and the burden of remembering all we have lost. And I doubt that I am alone in this hope balanced by cynicism.

I remember how outraged my late partner, David Lourea, was at the intrusion AIDS had made into his life. Eventually, frustrated and angry at the recurring beep reminding him to take his AZT, he threw his pillbox-timer against a wall, scattering his medication across the sidewalk. He never regretted the gesture, even saying it had made him feel better to strike out than be passive. The gesture was an angry one, but the anger let him feel alive and less like a victim. He held onto the hope that he might survive the epidemic even as he wrote his will and prepared for his death, even as I openly wept at the sight of his diminishing frame.

While I have survived him and most of the friends I had 12 years ago, I do not feel like a "survivor". Rather, I feel more like one who has been abandoned. In this I cannot be alone. Loneliness, missing our lovers and our friends, has become a second epidemic. We, the "survivors", are left bereft, grieving awake and asleep, and wondering if the dead are not the lucky ones after all. We ask ourselves: Do the dead feel the pain of loss, of separation? Or do they know the joy of reunion that different theologies and those who have had "near death experiences" would have us believe? None of us will know until we join them, of course, and there in is the invitation to despair and hope. Why not join the dead? is the often asked question. How many AIDS deaths are, after all, actually suicides? And as Stevie Smith pointed out, Death is the only god we can call at will. Taken in this light, suicide, as a final act of empowerment, is nothing if not appealing.

So often I feel like Viola, the heroine of **The Twelfth Night** who, having survived a shipwreck wonders about her brother's chances of survival. At one moment she resigns herself to his death, consigning him to Elysium, at the next dresses as a boy to make her way in Illyria in the hope of finding him. Similarly, I resign myself to my losses and retain my hope that there will be a medical breakthrough, that somehow I will be a survivor. But will survival be something to be envied?

David, a psychotherapist, once remarked to our Rabbi that if there were a cure tomorrow there would be an outpouring of unexpressed rage and grief that would consume us all, adding to the burden of survival. And then, he asked, what will be our job? How will we cope with the demands that we as survivors will make on each other? And how many so called "survivors" will, like uncounted holocaust survivors after World War II, unequipped to deal with the accumulated loss, take their own lives?

If being a long term survivor is a blessing, as some would have me believe, it also has a double edge. "Who will take care of me when you're gone?" I once asked David in tears. "I don't know," he answered. "I don't know. And I worry about it all the time." As time has passed, as I lose more and more of my friends (three within 10 days of each other last spring) the anxiety of survival swells within me. Who, I want to know, will be around to take care of me if I get sick? This is the question so often thought by myself and others but rarely spoken for fear of being judged. But it is a very real concern, an added weight.

I recently saw a play in San Francisco where in the only male character, a gay man with AIDS, is attended to by his lesbian friends as he dies. Having recently been released from the hospital myself, I identified with him instantly. Is he, like me, I asked myself, surrounded by lesbians because most, perhaps all, of his male friends are dead? Fortunately for me, I've always had lesbian friends, friends who stood by me through David's illness and eventual death, guarded and supported me as I grieved for my loss, and then attended to my needs through my protracted illness. One friend, was even prepared to postpone a trip to Italy for fear I'd die in her absence.

Along side these women was my oldest and best friend, Michael, one of the few male friends I have left from before the plague. Today when Michael and I get together, two widowers at the table, we still camp, still talk about food and sex with equal enthusiasm, still share the latest information on HIV treatment. But there remains the unspoken question: Will you survive me or will I survive you? And which fate is the worse? How would either of us cope without the other after 12-plus years of an intense and intimate friendship? With fewer and fewer friends to call on, we have both come to rely on each other more than before. And if Michael dies before me, I will be that character in the play, surrounded and attended to by women because there is no one else left. There are worse fates, to be sure, than to be attended to by loving friends, but it is men I love and their increasing absence from my life continually gnaws at my heart.

I am grateful for my friends and family, but so accustomed to death that I live in fear that anyone of them might die - of breast cancer, of AIDS, in an accident - and be lost to me. For, if it were not for them, survival would be a lost cause. When I die they will remember me, say *kaddish* for David and me, remember our *yartzheits*, and we will live on in their memories of us. But in the mean time, remembering the dead is my obligation. My brothers may be in Elysium, you see, but I am alive and, like all survivors, share with my friends the burden of remembering.

Life after Life:
Further Notes on Survival

Need and desire are, like cotton madras, inclined bleed.
– Fran Lebowitz

Widowhood sucks.

"It's a social aberration," a widowed friend told me. "Most of the world doesn't know what to do with widows or queers. Imagine being both?" Living in a world that marches two-by-two, I have since discovered that my friend was right. Even in this, the most enlightened of cities, there is a discomfort in the population at large. Those that felt they had achieved something in being accepting of the openly queer in the workplace now find themselves uncomfortable in the realization that queers have lives. While our own community comes to grip with the increasing numbers of AIDS widowers and breast cancer widows, there is still nothing to compare to the social awkwardness of being asked, "Single?" It was only after I started dating again, more than a year after my first husband had died, that I discovered a whole new set of hazards.

Finding sex was seldom a problem. Even the recently bereaved can fumble about with a stranger in a dark room. It wasn't even meeting people that I found problems. Offering the information that I was HIV-positive was, as often as not, greeted with "Me too." It was the information that I was widowed that frightened away so many members of the dating pool (which I'd already limited to HIV-positive men.) Too often to be coincidence, the response was an uneasiness that only added to my own. Interest was often lost the moment I revealed my marital status. Questions like, "Are you okay with it now?" (which I found particularly inane) were pressed upon me as if to measure the exact depth of my grief, and hence desirability.

Please understand, I was not crying on the shoulders of these men, nor did I introduce myself as a widower. I even made the conscious decision not to talk about my late spouse when I met new people. Perhaps it was just the knowledge that my life had once been shared for eight years with someone before, that I was only available now by reason of an epidemic, that frightened men away, superimposing the ghost of my late husband over any dinner conversation that we might attempt. Or, very possibly, I was just too frank in allowing that I still wanted and needed to be in love: needs are so unattractive on a first date.

On the opposite end of the spectrum were those anxious to be coupled against all odds, even before my husband had died. More than one acquaintance presented himself to me as a potential new spouse long before such a declaration was appropriate. I have since learned that others have shared the same experience. It is as if, having once been assessed as husband material (which a widower must perforce be), a claim was staked on my person. All very flattering, to be sure, but hardly the grounds for sharing a life together.

As jaded to life and death issues as the epidemic has made me, I remain an incurable romantic, one who fondles his affections the way others admire precious gems. I love courtship and all it entails: flowers, notes, chocolates and a better brand of condoms. I love candlelit dinners, schmaltzy music, burning glances, meaningful sighs, walks in the park: the whole gamut of romantic litter. To complicate matters further, my taste for the kind of sex that would shock most of America has only increased with the years, not lessened. So where does one find someone as romantic *and* kinky as oneself?

Well, damn if I hadn't known him for years. Yes, gentle reader, he was in my own backyard all along. But before Phil I made the mistake that many widowers (including a heterosexual uncle of mine) make: a hasty marriage.

Not that my error in judgment was such a bad guy, just too much too soon. That he courted me when I was needy enough to think myself in love is neither here nor there. That I mistook earth-shattering sex for love is the error I made and foolishly stuck to in spite of increasing evidence to the contrary. Later, as I sat among the ashes of what had been an intense affair, I believed that I would never be in love again, that the last bit of passion had been burned away. I feared that my heart would never skip a beat or my breath ever falter again. Imagine my relief to discover that my heart could still be reached, that I could remember the difference between love, need and desire – even when the three are so intricately linked.

Phil was more than an acquaintance, not quite a friend, and an occasional fuck buddy. That we were attracted to each other from the beginning is now well established. That he kept a respectful distance during David's illness and my subsequent grief would earn points with me when I discovered he'd been attracted to me sexually all along. It was really not until I heard him explaining to a mutual friend all he had to offer a spouse, a long list of virtues that no one had appreciated enough to snatch him up, that I asked myself, "Why am I not dating this man?"

It was with trepidation that I asked him out, not because I knew he would be my new husband, but because I was afraid to let myself be open to the possibility of loss again. As much as I wanted to fall in love again, I panicked at the thought of sharing my life with someone new. But how does one resist the attention of a man who brings flowers, sends notes, and knows how to kiss? How could I hold back when I so quickly grew accustomed to his body next to mind at night, his eager smile each time he came to spend the evening with me, to say nothing of his wicked sense of fun when we fucked? Thoughtful as he is nasty, it was not hard to fall in love, not to want to share a life with him.

Not that I am no longer afraid. Love can be as terrifying as it is exhilarating, and I already know from experience that the euphoria can only last so long before it is replaced by either a calm contentment or an annoying tedium. A comfortable couple is what I want us to be, what I see us evolving into already. It is also what we both want, to be a family, to share our friends and our lives, to know someone will be there should one of us fall ill, to be needed as well as to need. It's part of the human experience, something far too precious for words to capture with any accuracy, but something so necessary for many (perhaps even most) of us.

A few months before he died, my first husband, David, said that while he did expect me to be sad and to mourn after he died, he wanted me to fall in love again, to find someone new when I was ready.

"I won't," I said. "I can't see myself being with someone new ever."

"That's not true," he said. "You like being coupled too much. Just make sure it's someone I'd approve of – or I'll be back to haunt you."

We laughed after that, as we often laughed together, but I never forgot his words, and now I know he was right. I prefer life paired. Phil makes me laugh like David did, forces me to re-think some of my old ideas, argues intelligently over social issues, and (so important to a writer) knows how to appreciate what I write even when he criticizes it. But even as he fills so many of the gaps left by David, he is not David, does not try to be David, nor, to my credit, do I expect him to be David. They are very different from each other, yet share many of the same qualities I've come to value in a spouse. While Phil lacks most of David's annoying habits, he also has his own to contend with – as I do mine. While we are of different faiths, we share some of common beliefs and able to share those things with each other, and it is those shared beliefs, I am certain, that will carry us through the rocky times ahead.

Now, as he moves his belongings into our home, I'm filled with a different kind of fear. It is likely, perhaps even certain, that both of us will die young. We're both relatively healthy, but HIV-positive. It is likely that I, the older and living with fewer CD4 cells, will die first, but HIV is nothing if not insidious and has the annoying habit of progressing differently in each of its hosts. Nothing is certain for any of us in this world, of course, no matter what our HIV status, but one can't help but believe that the throw of the dice for HIV-positive people is loaded. It is a gamble worth taking, though, and life is too short for this man not to try. Loss is a part of life for everyone, even if it seems our community has had more than it's share, but there is no point in denying ourselves a chance at happiness, even when we know there is a good chance we will lose it. Or why bother living at all?

Hole:
A Sordid Sort of Memoir

Enravishment doesn't give meaning to life,
and yet without it life seems meaningless.
– Diane Ackerman

I'd already been given my birthday flogging.

At a monthly leather party a few nights before (one so well attended each month, despite it being on a school night, that it often reminds me of the old days), I'd been standing about minding my own business, when a man I'd never seen before approached me with the dog collar I knew on sight.

"You're David?"

"Yes..."

"You've seen this before?"

"Yes..."

He fastened the collar around my neck, slipped a finger through the D-ring and pulled me by it to another part of the former warehouse (now a sex club), and to where my lover, Phil, was waiting.

"David, this is my friend Paul," said Phil. "You can call him 'Sir.'"

"Yes, Sir."

"Lick his boots."

I obeyed.

Hole

As I licked the stranger's boots, Phil and Paul discussed me as if I weren't there, talking about types of bondage that might look aesthetic on my six-foot, one-hundred, ninety-pound frame, or whether or not I deserved to be fucked.

I was pulled from the stranger's boots to Phil's boots. I continued licking, still listening.

"He has a hood," Phil told Paul. "We should have brought it."

"Yeah? Bet it looks good on him."

After a few more minutes I was pulled to my feet and made to stand a foot away while they continued their conversation.

"Are you going to fuck him?"

"Maybe later. After he's beaten. It's his birthday this Sunday, so I want to give him a treat."

Not long after that I was shackled to a Saint Andrew's cross and ordered to count in the usual manner ("One, Sir! Two, Sir!" et cetera) while Phil whipped me. I obeyed, as always when collared. I felt the usual rush from the flogging, resulting in the usual hard-on when it was all over. Since it was my birthday in a few days, I was allowed to get off. I fastened the collar around my right boot, and in short order found a mouth eager enough to assist me. Splattering my cum all over my new friend's chest, I thanked him with a kiss and went looking for Phil. We left soon after that. After all, Phil had to work the next day.

Now it was Sunday, my actual birthday. I wondered what Phil had up his sleeve. Something was obviously up. There had been many phone calls from which I was excluded, many knowing looks between Phil and our friends. I had my suspicions.

I sat in the living room reading when he brought me a sandwich and a soda I hadn't asked for. Obviously, he had some activity planned that would prevent me from eating for a while. He didn't want me getting hungry in the middle of whatever was to come since he knew from experience that when my blood sugar drops, things get ugly

Half an hour later, Phil entered the room in leather and Levis smoking a cigar: Always a good sign. I would, at the very least, get fucked on my birthday.

"Don't you think you should change into something more comfortable?" he asked.

"Sure, Daddy. What should I...?"

"Why don't you go into the bed room and see what's there?"

I did as he suggested and found a pair of boots, a leather harness and my black leather briefs with the front to back zipper laid out for me. I put them on and went back to the living room.

"Very nice," he said. "Now my boots need licking."

I have had a boot fetish since I was a child. The sound of boots clicking on the sidewalk gave me a rush even before adolescence. At the age of eleven, I saw a biker drive by on the freeway with thigh-high boots, jeans, gloves and no shirt. I masturbated to the image for years to come. Licking boots, then, is a favorite activity of mine. Numerous men have demanded it of me, and I've never failed to respond with enthusiasm. As I groveled on all fours to obey Phil this time, he fastened the dog collar around my neck.

After Phil was satisfied with the condition of his boots, he took me to the bedroom where there were candles burning and the black synthetic play sheet had been put on the bed. I was laid face down on the bed. The back of my briefs was unzipped. Yes, I would be fucked. I felt his full weight on top of me as he grunted, filling me with his cock, finally cumming with the words, "Fuck you, fuck you!"

Sweet romance.

Done fucking me, he Fastened my wrists together with a pair of leather cuffs and secured those to the D-ring of my collar. Blind folding me, he said, "I have a few things to do now. You stay here and behave."

"Yes, Sir."

I stayed where he left me for some time, wondering what was next. He came in again, held my head in his hands and whispered, "I love you."

Before I could respond, the doorbell rang and he went to answer it, telling me to be good and stay put. I began to suspect what the evening was to hold for me.

Phil loves to see me get fucked by other men. He loves to tell me how my butt is his to give away. Our favorite memories of our last trip to Europe were going to backrooms in Amsterdam and London where Phil pulled down my Levis and told strangers to fuck me. While I was being fucked by these nameless men, Phil would lovingly whisper, "I'm giving your butt away." To which I could only respond, "Thank you, Sir."

Something of the same sort of activity seemed to have been planned for tonight.

A few minutes later Phil returned with someone else.

"This is my lover David," he said to the new arrival. "I just finished fucking him. David, this is a friend of mine. You can call him 'Sir.'"

"Yes, Sir."

"My friend is horny so I said he could fuck you."
"Yes, Sir."
"It's his birthday," he told the stranger.
"Happy birthday."
"Thank you, Sir."
"So you can fuck him," Phil continued to his friend. "Or do anything else you want. Because he's a hole. Isn't that right, hole?"
"Yes, Sir."
"See you," Phil told the stranger.
"Yeah, thanks."
My wrists were released from the collar, but the cuffs stayed on.
"You like to get fucked, hole?"
"Yes, Sir."
"Let's see how much you like it. Suck on this."
I reached out blindly with my mouth, floundering a moment before finding the fat cock being offered to me. I tried my best to suck it down, wrapping my lips around my teeth, using my tongue as best I could. Suddenly the cock was pulled away from me.
"Guess you don't really want it."
"Yes I do, Sir!"
"We'll see."
I felt my balls being pinched. Clothespins, I realized, were being fastened to my scrotum.
"What do you say?"
"Thank you, Sir."
Another was attached.
"And?"
"Thank you, Sir."
By the third clothespin, I knew what was expected of me, and after each clothespin was attached I responded appropriately. When he was satisfied with his work he told me to take a deep breath. The clothes pins were pulled off rapidly, making me cry out in pain as the blood rushed back.
"Thank you, Sir."
"Good boy. Now maybe you can suck this right."
This time the cock was shoved into my waiting mouth. I sucked dick with my best technique, working the fat hose into something stiff and hard. Eventually I choked trying to take the whole thing down.
I heard the sound of a camera; it's flash just bright enough to be seen from the edges of my blindfold.

Apparently pleased with my enthusiasm this time, especially since I'd choked on his dick, he pulled his cock from my mouth and stuck a greased finger in my butt hole. Then another. I moaned softly.

"How many do you think you can take, hole?"

"I don't know, Sir," I answered honestly. I'd never successfully been fisted, and it had been more than ten years since anyone had tried.

"Three, four?"

"I think so, Sir."

"My whole fist?"

"No, Sir. I've never been fisted, Sir."

"I see. How many fingers do you think are in there now?"

"Three, Sir?" I guessed.

"Try four."

"Thank you, Sir."

"Good boy," he said with a slap on my ass.

I felt each leg being lifted over his shoulders.

"Ready to get fucked?"

"Yes, Sir!"

He entered slowly, and then pounded away. I grunted, groaned with pleasure.

"Yes, Sir!" I cried. "Thank you, Sir!"

He paused a moment to undo my wrists.

"Now pinch my tits like a good boy," he said.

"Yes, Sir."

I heard Phil come into the room.

"See?" he asked his friend. "I told you he was a hole."

"I can see that."

He continued pounding into me. I continued to grunt and groan. I felt Phil's face next to mine. "I'm giving your butt away, David."

"Thank you, Sir."

The doorbell rang again.

"I wonder who that could be," said Phil. I heard him leave the room.

The man fucking me paused and I continued pulling on his nipples.

"What a fucking hole. You keep pinching my tits so you must want it bad."

"Yes, Sir!"

"Then grunt like a pig!" he commanded.

I felt his cock return to its earlier rhythm inside my ass hole. I grunted like a pig, or what I thought a pig would grunt like since I'd never actually heard one, as he used my hole.

I heard Phil return to the room just in time to see his friend shoot all over me. I heard him breath rapidly, then yell as I felt the hot cum splatter over my abdomen and chest.

"Come on," said Phil to his friend. "I'll get you something to drink. You look thirsty."

Phil refastened my wrists to my collar and they left the room.

A short time later the door opened again.

"David, another friend of mine is here with his boy. You can call them both 'Sir.' They're horny and I told them what a hole you are so... I guess their both going to fuck you."

"Yes, Sir."

The door closed and I heard the two men talking, one giving orders to the other.

"Open him up," ordered the daddy.

"Yes, Sir," I heard.

My wrists were detached from my collar and I was rolled over onto my stomach.

The new stranger, the boy, mounted my ass and proceeded to fuck me with sharp, hard strokes.

"I'm just getting you ready for my man," he said. "Then my daddy is gonna fuck you good. We hear you're a real hole."

"Yes, Sir."

A few minutes later we were interrupted.

"Now me," said the strange daddy.

I was mounted again, my arms held down against my waist.

"You like that, hole? Huh?" he grunted.

"Yes, Sir."

"Then talk to me!"

"It feels so good, Sir. Fuck me, Sir. Use my hole, Sir. Tear me apart with that big cock of yours, Sir."

"That's better."

The two men, daddy and boy, continued to fuck me, taking turns. It went on for what seemed like a long time.

Phil came in shortly after that with the first stranger. I could hear them having sex as I was being fucked. It only added to the heat. Again, I heard the sound of a camera's flash.

I heard the doorbell ring again. "Good," I thought. "It must be the pizza."

"You guys done yet," Phil finally asked.

"In a little bit,"

"Okay," said Phil. "Enjoy."

I heard Phil and the first man leave the room.

When the two men decided that they'd had their fill, the daddy whispered in my ear.

"Now you be careful", he said with a nasty chuckle. "The man that fucks you next might not be as gentle as me."

I lay for a while on the bed alone, covered in sweat and cum, wondering what was next. Apparently it wasn't pizza.

The door opened. Phil came in with more "friends."

"David, it looks like all my friends are horny tonight, so I said they could fuck you too. Now one of them is big hairy bear with a really big cock. Is that okay?"

"Yes, Sir!"

"And you'll be a good hole?"

"Yes, Sir!"

I heard Phil leave the room.

"So it's your birthday, today?" a deep voice asked.

"Yes, Sir."

"How many men have had your hole tonight, birthday boy?" asked the second.

"Four so far, Sir."

"Having a good birthday, hole?" asked the first.

"Yes, Sir!"

"How many times have you come so far?"

"Not once, Sir."

"Oh? When will you come?"

"When Daddy says I can."

This answer seemed to please them. I heard a chuckle of approval from both of them.

My legs were lifted over a pair of broad, strong shoulders. My hands wondered up the hairy torso and broad chest.

"Like that?"

"Yes, Sir."

"Like this?"

He rubbed the biggest cock I'd felt in years between my legs.

"Fat like a Coke can, huh? And when it comes, it's gonna shoot right against your prostate."

"Yes, Sir!"

There was no ceremony or warm-up this time. No greased fingers preparing me for what was to come. He shoved the huge monster inside of me. I almost came. If I'd been allowed to touch myself, I would have shot all over his hairy chest right then and there.

"Like that?"

"Yes, Sir."

"You like it like *this*?" He slammed his cock hard inside me.

"Yes, Sir," I gasped.

"Good!"

He continued slamming inside of me, punch fucking me with his big dick.

"Yes, Sir! Yes, Sir! Yes, Sir!"

Again, I've no idea how long this actually went on. Eventually Phil came back into the room with the others. He undid my wrist restraints, and, as if to punish me for this relative freedom, the stranger pulled out of me.

I felt the bed sway as the complete group of men got on it with me. There were grunts and groans, the sound of skin being stroked. They were jerking off all over me. One by one I felt each man's load splatter over me.

"You too," said Phil. "Shoot us a big birthday load."

There is something about being commanded to come that makes it hard for me to come – performance pressure I guess. Nervously, I pulled on my dick, felt the gold ring in my cock between my greasy fingers. I was hard almost at once. Strange hands caressed me, pulled on my pierced tits, and fingered my asshole. I shot my load. I was relieved when I came, not wanting to appear ungrateful to the nameless men who had just fucked me just so I could have this very special birthday. Though I was disappointed that the last of Phil's "friends" hadn't also fucked me. I guess he just liked to watch his lover fuck.

There were a variety of sloppy kisses exchanged between the others and me. Cum was rubbed all over me, mixed with sweat. Then they left the room. Phil threw a towel at me, still blindfolded, and shut the door. I heard him talk to the others, offering them the shower and clean towels as I wiped myself off.

Phil's "friends" came in one or two at a time to wish me happy birthday again.

"But you don't know who we are, do you?" asked one.

"No, Sir."

"So you could be anywhere, at the Eagle or at party with your daddy, and wonder if one the guys who stops to say hello fucked you tonight?"

"Yes, Sir."

"But you won't know, will you?"

"No, Sir."

He left the room laughing.

Sometime later I heard the front door slam as the last of our guests left. Phil came in, took off the blindfold and kissed me.

"I don't know about you," he said. "But I worked up an appetite."

"Thank you, Daddy."

"I love you, David."

"I love you."

"Good. Now take a shower while I make us some supper."

I got up on wobbly legs, looked at the waste basket next to the bed filled with used condoms and latex gloves, and wondered how, or if, I'd ever walk again after such an assault.

"You know," I said as Phil took off my collar. "You don't have to wait for a special occasion if you ever want to do this again."

"Hole."

We kissed again, long and deep.

Sweet romance.

Falling into the Cyber Dungeon

How am I to manipulate this mass of crystallized data in order to work out the meaning of it and so give the coherent picture of this impossible city of love and obscenity?
– Lawrence Durrell

Until this moment I'd never done more than use e-mail or look up the weather on the other coast before flying east. But being smarter than the average bear, and a pervert to boot, once I started snooping around on the web, it wasn't long before I stumbled on some like minded folks in the Cyber Dungeon. Finding it didn't take long at all, actually, at least not from the moment I started sniffing my away around cyber space, proving that the combination gaydar and my inveterate nose for sleaze can be put to good use anywhere – even along the information highway.

Way back when, when I was not much more than a boy and a novice pervert anxious to experience everything and anything available in my *demi monde* of choice, I'd been fortunate enough to fall into a group of women and men, most of them queer, a few of them transgendered, all them twisted, who made up the population of the SM parties I attended at the now legendary Catacombs. The most amusing part of my evenings at the Catacombs with this tattooed and pierced, leather and rubber clad, cross dressed and corseted family of friends were my interactions outside the playroom. It was here at the bar where a matronly dominatrix talked about her new slave boy's love of being paddled, where a statuesque MTF demanded I kiss her boots to compensate for being such a smart ass bottom, where my date for the evening gave me my diet soda in a dog dish, and where I was occasionally threatened with some very real punishments by menacing tops fed up with my bad boy attitude, should I dare step into the dungeon unescorted. In short, a good time was had by all as our assorted personas (some of them as mutable as putty) met and meshed deep into the wee hours of the morning. I thought I was in heaven.

But what I was experiencing was just the last hurrah of a once vital era. A year or so later the Catacombs closed, and it would be several more years before I'd find another collection of jaded and decadent souls who'd be as warm and supportive as the clan I had met at the Catacombs. Even this second clan would pass away as too many friends, male and female, were taken from us by a plague that was hell bent on ruining a good thing. What I once had, then, I missed, and had pretty much given up hope of finding again. That is, until I fell (not quite by accident) into the Cyber Dungeon.

The first time I chanced into the Cyber Dungeon I arrived in the middle of a rather animated discussion about tops: Who was the better, meaner, hotter, nastier top, men or women? Never one to be shy when it came giving out opinions (since I have so many of them) I immediately piped in with my own observations. Pointing out first that being a fag I usually played with men and only occasionally bottomed to women, and that those women were always lesbians, I said that female tops seem less invested in nurturing their bottoms than male tops, almost as if they were tired of being nurturers and just wanted to hurt somebody.

I sent this little commentary out into cyber space to be answered: "Very good. LOL."

"LOL? I queried. Is that good?"

"LOL = Laughing out loud," someone thoughtfully answered for me.

Discovering a moment later that I could look up profiles on these folks, I set out to do just that, and came to discover that I was the only guy there in the dungeon. Well, being an honorary lesbian of some standing, and quite used to being the only boy at the party, I stayed, chatting with the women, making insightful and (I was certain) witty observations to be told again and again: LOL.

Looking up at the clock an hour later, I saw that I needed to get dinner ready soon, and excused myself from the ladies I was attending with the words:

See you later! Have to get Daddy his dinner!

After signing off I saw how one could get hooked on this.

The next time I entered the Cyber Dungeon I found myself in the middle of a scene, one where in two women (both dominatrix, as I was later to learn) were threatening each other with knives and riding crops. A moment after I entered, a woman from the east coast informed me with a **[whisper]** that a really hot scene was taking place and that everyone was just watching for the moment. I of course thanked her with a **[whisper]** and looked to see who else was in the dungeon.

Right at this moment a message appeared at the top of the screen, a special message for me from someone I'd never heard of. I looked up his profile before answering. Ah, I learned, another San Francisco leather man looking for some action.

So I responded:

Hey. Do I know you?

He answered:

Not yet. Maybe we can get together, though.

To make a long story short, he turned out to be a bottom *and* my senior. Now while I am a switch by nature as well as nurture, I don't usually top significantly older guys. It doesn't feel right, so I don't do it. Not wanting to tell him this for fear of being thought ageist, which I suppose I was in fact being, I said that I was exclusively a bottom as well, excused myself and went back to the dungeon.

By this time, the women had gone off together and I was left with an assortment of men and women not unlike those I had once known in the Catacombs. With handles that translated into titles like Mr. Leather Daddy, She Who Must Be Obeyed, Boy Cadet, or Premier Dominatrix of the Cosmos, the individuals settled easily into their roles in the Cyber Dungeon. Each cyber pervert let the others know what was going on by describing the action in cyber space, usually in the third person present, with phrases like **[kneeling at Daddy Bear's feet]** or **[submissively handing Mister Man his riding crop]** or **[hanging head in shame]** or my favorite **[crossing her legs and resting her stiletto-heeled feet on Lowly Worm's back.]**

This was certainly *my* kind of crowd.

As I spent more time in this cyber *demi monde*, I got to know a lot of folks I was chatting up in the dungeon. The SM etiquette of the Old Guard was often kept, something I hadn't seen since the Catacombs. Submissives spoke only to each other unless spoken to by a Dominant. A Master or Mistress might give an order to a submissive that would then **[run to obey.]** I was getting a rush from all this, goose bumps rose all over my skin as I nostalgically offered to **[lay flat on my stomach to better service Mr. Biker Cop's knee high boots]** as my old fetish for law men in uniform once again emerged.

Looking at the profiles of the guys I met on line, I more than once came across men who at least claimed to be police or highway patrol officers. As in phone sex, people can say anything about themselves, of course, and some of the cyber perverts I met certainly had more than one handle, that is to say more than one persona, as they waltzed in and out of the Cyber Dungeon door. So I never knew for certain if Mr. Biker Cop was really what he claimed, no more than I could be certain that the leather boy stud muffin in north east Pennsylvania claiming to be "29 YO GWM w/ 30" waist, 46" chest, washboard abs" in his profile was all he professed to be either, but neither did I care. This was all fantasy, after all. And it was fun. So when Mr. Biker Cop entered the dungeon, and as I had hoped still in his uniform, I noted that his boots were dusty and asked if he'd like them cleaned off. Being agreeable, he said I could but only if I used my tongue.

Well, duh!

While others in the Cyber Dungeon chatted between themselves, I occasionally interjected a **[lick, slurp, lick]** just to remind them that I was still there and doing what I do best. When I was done with his boots I asked what else needed serviced. Too my joy, he suggested we go into a private room of the Cyber Dungeon to continue our little scene. Clearly, Mr. Biker Cop was an officer *and* gentleman.

Then there was the time I as minding my own business doing some actual work on line (checking out Eurail Schedules for next summer's trip) when I suddenly saw another message on my screen:

Do you paddle guys?

This seemed like a reasonable question to me, but before I answered him I looked up his profile: A twenty-something fly-boy from the north. This sounded good to me, so I answered, honestly enough:

Yes. And I also cane and flog guys, too. Why? Have you been bad?

As I suspected, he had been bad. Further more, he needed a stern talking to before being punished, all of which sounded like fun to me. One thing led to another as I continued to look up the Channel Tunnel weekend train schedule with one hand while I answered Spank Me Boy's questions with the other: How long had I been paddling guys? What kind of paddles did I have? Could we get together when he was in San Francisco?

To my surprise we made a date to meet a few weeks hence. He signed off with the words:

By the way, I have a cute butt.

Okay, I thought. I can live with that. Cute butts are good.

By now I had figured out that there was a way to look up others on-line by interest, and since my profile mentioned leather, and that my primary fetishes were cigars, boots and gloves, I was attracting some attention just by being on-line and open about my sexual quirks. At about this time, I received another message, this time from Bay Area Boot Boy. This fellow started his overtures with a simple:

What's up?

This left me the opportunity to check out his profile and discover that he was thirty-something fellow with a particular fondness for Dehners boots. (Well, who doesn't like Dehners boots, I'd like to know?)

After some small chat, I started talking about my own Dehner's, about how high they were, how in need of polishing they were, about how I'd like to lay back and smoke a cigar while someone took care of them... You get the idea. And so, another date was made.

Where was Daddy Sir through all this, you ask? Quietly watching me with amusement as I made plans to fill the evenings he had classes.

"Just don't forget the way home," he said when I told him about my plans to meet these men.

"Of course not," I replied with the smart ass tone that can, if I play my cards right, sometimes get me a spanking. "I just want the chance to top once in a while."

"Fine," he said sipping his coffee as he read the newspaper. "There's not much of a chance of our needing you to do that here."

So much for getting my butt spanked; he spanked my ego instead. I hate it when he's right. From his response, though, it was clear that I couldn't spend too much time in the Cyber Dungeon if I was hoping to get what I wanted from the man I love.

All this time in cyber space is just a bit of fun on the side. But maybe other people can find true love on the web, or even the sort of relationship they want in the Cyber Dungeon. Anything seems possible. As with personal ads, the more specific and honest one is, the better one's chances of meeting someone special, especially if one is searching for love. If it's just sex, though, honesty is probably about as welcome as it is in phone sex where fantasy rules. Just as it is with any new toy, how much good we get out of meeting places like the Cyber Dungeon will depend on how we use it and what we want to get out of it. As for me, being in the Cyber Dungeon seems a lot like the old days at the Catacombs: A good time is being had by all.

I Bought the Plot – *Now What?*

People who are afraid of living are also especially afraid of death.
  – Médard Boss

"You need to plan for your future," my doctor told me as he came into the examining room. Stunned at his greeting, it was not until later that I also heard the implied, but unspoken words, "now that you have a future."

At a later appointment he admitted that he had lied to me three years earlier, back when I weighed a third less than I do now and had a CD4 count of 70. Filling out the viatical applications that would allow me to sell my life insurance, he'd written that my life expectancy was about 18 months. "I'm just saying that to them," he had assured me then. "I actually expect you to live much longer." Now he conceded that he had told them the truth and lied to me. Quite honestly he hadn't expected to see me three years hence, remarkably fit, still going to the gym, with a CD4 count of around 1000.

Damn, I thought. This means I'm going to have to pay off those credit cards after all.

And what about the plot I'd paid for, the one next to my first lover, back when I thought my life was over and I'd never fall in love again? And how would my second husband feel about burying me next to my first, especially now that there was no room left for him should he care to join us?

"S'okay," he assured me when I brought this up. "I'm going to be cremated anyway."

Okay, but what about all the home care equipment I have stored in the garage, like the shower chair, the donut pillow and the sharps container? What should I do with all that stuff now? Holding on to it seemed silly, but getting rid of it felt like asking for the Evil Eye. Dare I presume on my good fortune?

I never expected to have these problems, but now that I have them, I find them peculiarly refreshing. These are the problems of a PWA who is – maybe going to around a while? Which makes me nervous because I have this theory about long-term survivors. As soon as they appear in the media, make themselves known in some public forum like a conference or TV documentary, saying that they have too much to live for and plan on being around for a long, long time: They die.

I'm not making this up. I've seen it again and again. Quite literally, it's the kiss of death. So I wonder, why tempt the Powers That Be and proclaim my good standing among the living? After all, I may have slipped the Angel of Death's attention until now, so why remind him/her of my existence? Maybe if I just sit quietly with my normal CD4 count and low viral load not saying anything, s/he'll continue to forget all about me and I can go on like this indefinitely?

Then again, neither do I want to appear ungrateful for this amazing chance to see my god daughter reach adulthood, to see the next millennium after all, or to make yet another "last trip" (the third in as many years) to Europe. Dare I suggest to my husband that we save our money an extra year and not travel in 1998, so we can go to Australia for New Year's Eve 1999? Dare I tempt the Fates like this?

Damn right.

I'd been in a control group (just getting the usual antiretrovirals) in a protocol at the National Institutes of Health in Bethesda for about a year when I got so sick that my friends were (unbeknownst to me at the time) looking for new homes for my cats and dog. (Ironically, the illness turned out to be what is commonly called cat scratch fever which, while not an AIDS-related opportunistic infection, didn't manifest the expected systems because I was immune compromised, thus eluding diagnosis for four months. I made medical history by being the fourth such documented case. Just the same, though, I'd rather have not made the journals.) When I recovered and regained enough of my strength to return to the NIH, I was offered the opportunity to leave the control group and try Interluken 2. My CD4 count being around 70, I was not offered a lot of hope, but it was worth a try.

I can't explain how horrible treatment is with IL2. Hooked up to a pump for 23 hours a day for five days running my body was flooded with the drug, giving me a rash, nausea that was untouched by any combination of anti-nausea drugs, anorexia, diarrhea, and general misery. A month later, however, my CD4 had jumped to around 200, a count I could quite literally live with for some time. Then another drug, a protease inhibitor that had not yet been given final approval was added to my "cocktail." Even with the IL2 dose eventually being cut in half to something I could manage with the assistance of just a few other medications to control the side effects, the addition of the protease inhibitor pushed my CD4 up to 500 over the next few months. My IL2 treatments were eventually decreased from every other month to every third, and now to every fourth month.

More than that, where once I was ready to give up (I had purchased that plot, after all) I am now stable, healthy, and hungry for life. When one of the resident doctors at the NIH asked me my secret I told her, quite frankly, that I'd fallen in love again. Wise doctor that she is, she doesn't dismiss this variable from the formula. Married men, as we all know, live happier, healthier and longer lives than bachelors.

"I'm the IL2 poster boy," I told my sister, who also happens to be a doctor and an epidemiologist.

"Yes," she agreed. "But with small print on the bottom of the poster. You know: Results not typical. Individual results will vary."

She of course had read the reports on the protocol in the medical journals and knew my results were exceptional enough for NIH doctors to want to use me as an example whenever possible for their presentations. Talking to my sister I suddenly remembered what Quentin Crisp had said when Dick Cavet asked him what he had wanted to be when he was a little boy. "An invalid," Crisp answered with a wave of his hand. "I had quite a flair for it, you know." Could I, I now wondered, make a career of being the IL2 poster boy?

Which brings me to yet another problem. I did have a career once, of course, that I gave up to better enjoy those "last 18 months." I only decided to go on disability – almost a full year after I qualified for it – because I didn't want to spend the last years of my life working. Now, other than a little neuropathy and semi-regular bouts of fatigue that only last a day or so, I would probably be considered able bodied. Except that I'm afraid to go back work. To continue with the protocol at the NIH would mean working part time, which would mean no insurance. To go back to work full time would mean discontinuing the protocol, which would mean a slipping CD4 count and a rising viral load, which would ensure my once again returning to disability. You see my quandary: It's the unintended catch 22 built into the system that didn't take situations like mine into consideration because they hadn't been heard of before this. Again, though, it's great to have a problem like this to mull over.

Part of the problem is that I do disability so well. I don't understand the guys who stop working, become depressed, and spend their days watching TV in dark room. I have more to do now than I ever did. I don't know how I could go to work full time and still take care of everything I need to do. I don't even know how I did it all before. My days have structure. I make lists each morning to be sure I run all my errands, keep all of my appointments, and take care of things around the house. This domestic life is also how I got well again, how I kept waking up each morning with pleasure at the prospect of a new day, how I was able to rest when I needed to, exercise when I was able to exercise, and to build a life with my new husband.

Maybe I'm afraid of letting it go because I'm afraid ill health will return when I return to the workplace. Or perhaps it all goes back to that fear of the Evil Eye. If I go back to work, it's like saying I'm well now, thus bringing me to the attention of those Fates one wants to avoid tempting. What if I go back to work and get sick again? For some reason, the prospect frightens me. It requires another leap of faith, like the first time I renewed a magazine subscription for two years instead of just one (which I now do all the time.) So I am summoning up the courage to make that leap, to find the right situation that will let me continue at the NIH while working and once again getting medical insurance.

What I won't do, though, is sell that plot. That would only be asking for trouble. It would be like needing something only after it's been thrown out. Only worse. Besides, I think as long as I never take any day for granted and treat this second chance at life with all due respect, the Fates will leave me alone for a while. Selling the plot though would be like spitting right in the old Evil Eye. Call this superstition if you want, but I'd rather be safe than sorry.

How I Fell in with the Wrong Crowd

*Regret is an appalling waste of energy,
and no one who intends to be a writer can afford to indulge in it.
– Katherine Mansfield*

I was walking to the gym one fine September day when I ran into my friend Roger walking with a man I'd not met before. When Roger Introduced us, his friend looked at me doubtfully and said that he thought he'd heard of me somewhere. "You've read David's stuff in *Drummer*," Roger thoughtfully interjected for me. Roger's friend looked me up and down, obviously dissatisfied with my tennis shoes, beach shorts and Gap T-shirt. "You're not what I expected," he said. "No," laughed Roger. "David never is what people expect."

This has long been the bane of my life: No one takes me seriously as a pervert. The problem is no doubt rooted in the reality that I am now, as I have ever been, a nice boy from a good family. Growing up, when others cited their life's goals, to be a doctor, nurse, lawyer, peace officer, businessman or clergy person, I knew only that I wanted to be jaded, to be part of a *demi monde* I was certain existed, even if I was still clueless as to what it was exactly, or where I'd find it. I discovered it in time, of course: a trip to Fire Island was my key.

During the summer of 1979, over a long weekend spent with little sleep and much prowling through the notorious meat rack, I watched with fascination as a leatherman humiliated, spat on, struck and eventually fucked a succession of pretty boys over as many nights. I stood back, feigning detachment each night, watching the scene unfold, and jerking off later to the remembered images. On my last night playing in the bushes (where over four nights I managed to do many things I'd never thought I'd do), the leatherman nodded at me, perhaps remembering me from previous nights' audiences, perhaps anticipating my participation. I ran off, inwardly screaming, terrified of what he must have recognized in me.

I would tell this tale in the years to come as an anecdote, an example of my nascent Puritanism. Being the product of a dozen generations of New England Puritans, I think now that the need to cast off that part of my heritage remains a motivating force for my sexual explorations. Indeed, I discovered in my journeys that the most enthusiastic perverts are inevitably from repressive (usually religious) backgrounds.

It was not until I casually mentioned to a date, after we'd had some pretty tremendous sex, that I liked getting spanked while getting fucked, that the journey really began. He obliged me on our next date by bending me over his knee and spanking me, asking me if I liked it. I of course answered in the affirmative. "Yes!" he asked. "Yes what?"

At that moment came clarity. Here was the answer, safely packaged in a man I knew and trusted, one I hadn't even known until that moment was kinky. He took me forward in small steps at first, bringing in new elements into each encounter. When he first stuck his boot in my face and told me to kiss it, he expected me to balk but I didn't. I fell forward in gratitude and was amply rewarded for my obedience with further humiliations and servitude.

Despite a series of obliging boyfriends and eager masters that followed (one of whom took an especial pleasure in plying me with drinks and then refusing his permission when I asked to use the men's room, just so he could punish me with diapers when I eventually wet myself), I knew that I'd truly arrived when I was invited to the Catacombs. The Catacombs was *the* kinky sex club in San Francisco. One could only attend a play party (as their bacchanalias were euphemistically called) if one were invited or had been brought by a member. With that invitation, a potential member had to know a member who could vouch for him (or her). My attendance that first Friday night at the Catacombs, then, was my final entrance into the world I'd been looking for since adolescence. The initiation I expected was not so horrific, at least not to one who'd already earned his bruises. My date collared and beat me as others had done before him, guiding me through the public displays of humiliation with an experienced hand. My enthusiasm made me (I only later realized) a minor star in the constellation of hot bottoms circling, and vying for the attention of, the much smaller and more elite cluster of tops.

One night, giving up on a boyfriend who was withholding sex to test my fidelity (a rather pointless test to assign to a self-described slut), I met and went home with a man some six and a half feet tall and proportionately well hung. Laying me on my stomach he prepared to enter me, murmuring something like, "Don't worry. Daddy will give it to you nice and easy." Disappointed to be cast into the role of innocent, and afraid that the man would not give me the kind of sex I wanted, I turned my head and said, "Don't be afraid of hurting me." Taking me at my word, he fucked me rough and hard, talking a line of trash that I'd never heard before, a menu of obscene fantasies that provoked even my jaded *libido*. He was the Daddy and I was the boy threatened with abuse if I didn't cooperate with his assault, but promised an ice cream if I pleased him. This from a man with a doctoral in music.

He ran the same monologue each time we played, striking nerves in me that sent me over the edge, both turned on and afraid. To my disappointment, however, despite how much he promised, or how ruthless the fuck, he never bought me that ice cream cone. When it was over we returned to our real selves, eliminating any chance of taking the fantasy out of the bedroom. As good as the sex was, his line was just a line, and he had no intention of acting any of it out with me in public. I would need to seek for that elsewhere.

This I learned was a common dilemma. Many of the men I met would talk a good line as we fucked, promising any number of sadistic fantasies, but all for their own benefit. I learned not to anticipate follow-up from these men, who were, after all, often no more than a quick fuck in the corner of a dark room.

To be fair to those who cast me as an innocent, I *did* work the boyish charm for as long as I could get away with it. Dressing in khaki walking shorts, a polo shirt and moccasins, I'd shyly cruise men in leather posing on their motorcycles on Castro Street. More than once I was motioned over with a "Come here, little boy." Whatever expectation he had of my being an inexperienced *naïf* was quickly shot to hell to reveal a butt that was black and blue from my date the night before

When playing that particular game at the Catacombs, however, I found the men who would walk the talk, men I could explain my needs to and be met with understanding, even enthusiasm. Though I find it hard to believe, even now, there was apparently a shortage of boys willing to be taken out on a leash.

One of the men I encountered at the Catacombs would in fact lead me down that chosen pathway, and on a leash. That he enjoyed seeing me lick his boots at many and assorted leather bars (and all to the consternation of the inevitable tourists) and kept me in shackles much of the time was all very well, but these little acts of affection were nothing compared to the nerves he struck when we were alone. One night, after the usual humiliation, beating my butt black and blue, and sexual subservience, he held me close in bed and whispered affectionately: "Now if you don't tell anyone about our private little games, we can play them forever…" A shiver ran up and down my spine. A feeling of unease settled into the pit of my stomach. My cock, meanwhile, was rock hard.

To had to the perversity, and hence my enjoyment, of the scene (which lasted from about 6 PM to around noon the next day) he put me in front of the television the next morning, a porno tape in the VCR, saying: "Time for Scooter's cartoons!" This was when I was finally allowed to jerk off – as he made us breakfast. Scooter, his special name for me, was embossed on a slave collar he gave me for Christmas. I added it to the collection of collars I'd received over the years, much in the same way Mae West collected diamonds from her admirers. The relationship with this wonderful man – Master and slave, Daddy and boy – might have gone on much longer if he hadn't queered it by falling in love with me at a time when I was unprepared for commitment.

Another man I met frequented San Francisco on business. I told him that I wanted to be bent over his knee and spanked, to which he readily agreed. He, like so many others, bought me a collar and walked me on a leash through the maze of alleys South of Market Street. He took special pleasure in making me drop my pants and pulling down my underwear (tidy whities that I always wore when with him since this was an especial fetish of his) and spanking me there in the deserted alley. My favorite part of our encounters was meeting him at his hotel. I would announce myself at the front desk. The receptionist would call his room to say, "There is a young man here to see you." "Send him up," was the reply. "He's my son." The receptionist, of course, assumed I was a callboy, an impression I reinforced with my choice of torn up jeans and leather jacket.

It was also at the Catacombs that I met my first partner, David Lourea. David was handsome, warm, loving and demented. Everyone wanted him, but I was the lucky one who had him for almost eight years. Like his predecessors, David enthusiastically flogged and humiliated me, used me sexually, but added his own special twist, murmuring to me in Yiddish, his first language. I jerked off in his arms while he called me *sheyna boychick*. I ate it up.

I suppose the apex (or perhaps the nadir, depending on how one looks at it) of it all came when David and I were invited to a straight SM wedding, one wherein the groom was brought in, naked, collared and bound. The guests were for the most part professional dominatrix – and to the last one, women who loved their work. The only male couple, there, we gathered a bit of attention during the reception. Collared and leashed, naked except for boots, gloves and leather briefs, I was kept on all fours and assigned the task of supporting the guest book on my straight back as it was signed. To the delight of all, I kissed the stiletto-heeled feet of the bride as I passed her in the reception line, offering my congratulations to the groom with a nod. I was greeted over and over again by the female guests with a pat on the head and "What a cute little puppy! Want mama to spank?"

Many years later, widowed and remarried, my sex life continues much the same. For our shared enjoyment, Sir puts me on a leash in leather bars, whips me into euphoria, fucks me when it pleases him and calls me his "boy." He also likes pulling my pants down in sex clubs and back rooms and telling strange men to "fuck my boy." This is one of my favorite activities, and it's not just the fucking, as pleasurable as it is. It's the humiliation of not knowing whose dick is inside me, of seeing the spilled lube and sperm accumulate on the floor. For my last birthday, he arranged a gangbang by a host of men I still can't identify since I was bound and blindfolded the whole time. It was one of the most romantic evenings of my life.

When recounting so much perversity, there is the obvious temptation to analyze. Perverts have learned, however, that while analysis can sometimes explain a sexual kink, it changes neither the need nor the desire for it. Most of us enjoy sex for a multitude of reasons, after all, not the least of which is fun. As with any fun activity, it is only natural that some people will cultivate the pleasure it provides. "Why" is a far less interesting pursuit than "how" or "what." In the end, it is feeling safe and warm in Sir's arms at night that really matters. The rest is just gravy.

Looking for Venice

If I'm a romantic, it's because I grew up watching old movies and treating them like real life. Glamour, I decided in my youth, was my natural element, and I was determined to wear it nobly – like Rosiland Russel in **That Velvet Touch** – as an example to the world. Furthermore, I intended to travel like they did in old movies, with steamer trunks and servants aboard glorious ocean liners. Alas, life's cruel lessons wiped most of these ideas from my head before I even got to college. Yet it was in college that I saw so many more old movies at the local art cinema (owned by a gay man, of course) and, on seeing Katherine Hepburn in **Summertime** for the first time, formed my idea of what Venice must be like – as well what I wanted my first visit there to be.

It didn't happen for almost twenty years, and when it did, my dreams were at once dashed by the reality of Venice in the 1990s. But only at first. It took a while, but my fantasy of Venice was eventually fulfilled as I sought to find what remained of the Venice that Hollywood had shown me, the romantic core of what remains one of the world's most beautiful cities.

My husband Phil and I were on our honeymoon. We arrived by train, looking anxiously for the long bridge across the lagoon that would bring us to Santa Lucia Station, the one Katherine Hepburn leaned out the train window to photograph. Somehow it wasn't quite as pretty as it was in the movie, the bridge (relatively new when the movie was made) having accumulated forty years worth of grime.. Nor was the lagoon as pristine as we had hoped despite the warnings of friends.

Hauling our bags to the *vaporetto*, I was nearly overwhelmed by the crowds of people, even in May when we had hoped to avoid the worst of the summer crowds. Still, despite the crush of tourists we managed to find seats with room for our bags (too many bags since, still longing for the age of steamer trunks and public porters, I always over pack.) It was then, sitting down and looking out the grimy, sea sprayed windows of the *vaporetto* that I glimpsed the Venice I hoped to see, beautiful even in it's decay, a little world unto itself.

Being a lover of maps, I already had three maps of Venice that I'd brought with me. Being well prepared, we got off at the right quay, Santa Maria del Giglio, and found our way to the small hotel another gay couple had recommended to us. We're it not for the sign on the main street, we might have missed the narrow alley that led us to the Hotel Flora and its lovely courtyard garden, but there it was and we fell in love with it at once. Still, it wasn't the lovely, spacious pension Kate stayed in in the movie, the home of a widow and graced with views of the canals at every turn.

Our room was small but adequate with a disproportionately large Venetian glass chandelier hanging over the bed. Our window looked down over the courtyard, which was nice enough, and probably for the best since Phil finds too much light obtrusive, especially first thing in the morning before he's had his coffee.

We found to our delight that Venice is even smaller than it appears in the maps. The hotel was only moments from the Ponte dell'Accademia in one direction, and the Piazza San Marco in the other. Meandering our way through the narrow streets, the *piazza* jumped out at us in a blaze of sunlight from the shadowed, narrow alley we were walking through. This was the moment of truth for us – well, for me anyway. I wanted /expected to see elegant people sitting in the outdoor cafes lining the square in the late afternoon, or a flock of pigeons fly into the air while young lovers ran across the square hand in hand. What we saw instead were hordes of tourists, mostly American and Japanese, in tour groups. Each cluster of tourists followed a guide carrying a flag, or a banner, or an aerial with a fake flower attached to it, to signal to his or her own particular throng to follow. I ached with disappointment.

Was the Venice of movies a lie, or had it vanished to make way for the tourism industry, an industry that it in fact needs to sustain itself? I remembered a college professor telling me years before that Venice had been ruined and that tourists had become its *raison d'etre*. I had also read that fewer and fewer people were able to live in Venice because it was too expensive to live in city whose only growing industry, tourism, depended on seasonal, low-wage workers.

These thoughts were made all the more certain when we saw a line of gondolas, ten in a row and looking like a ride at Disneyland, make their way up the canal. From our vantage on the bridge we heard an American woman impatiently ask the *gondolier*, "How long is this going to last?" As was more and more true all over the world, Venice's charms were being wasted on the masses. This, of course, is democracy's only drawback: Everyone's invited.

Too disappointed for words, we turned back towards our hotel.

"I want it to be the Venice we saw in **Summertime**," I sighed. "I want it to be..."

"You want it to be exclusive," inserted Phil, understanding me perfectly as usual, if a little better than I might like. "Maybe it will be different tonight when the day trippers are gone," he offered.

"Really?" I asked, aghast. "People come here just for the day?"

"Sure they do. The concierge told me while I was waiting for you downstairs. Tour groups rush in and out in an afternoon. Maybe tonight after dinner when it's less crowded it will be more like the movie."

"Maybe..."

Walking to dinner that evening we managed to get lost, which is a part of the experience in Venice, after all. Shops were closing, and the crowds had dwindled. The further away we got from the Piazza San Marco, the less crowded it became. The shops lining the narrow streets also became more interesting. Looking into store windows I saw wonderful art glass, not the junky trinkets in the gift stalls on the *piazza*. There were stationary shops filled with marbled paper books, fancy pens and sealing wax, and hand printed writing paper. Little galleries overflowed with beautiful etchings and framed prints. I perked up somewhat, my mood improved by the prospect of smart shops filled with gorgeous things.

Later that night, after dinner, we took a rambling walk through the still, warm evening. Other strollers were out enjoying the evening, as well, but it was far from crowded. Wandering aimlessly, we ended up, by a rather circuitous route, at the Ponte dell'Accademia. Standing at the top of the bridge, we looked out over the city, the full moon reflected in the Grand Canal. Phil put an arm around me and stole a kiss.

"Is this better?" he asked, ever solicitous.

"Much," I said. "Now it's a lot more like the movie."

"But not *just* like it?"

"Of course not. Real life can't be like movies. I just wish it would play that way."

We walked back to the Hotel Flora, finishing our after dinner cigars in silence.

Meals in Venice, we had discovered that night, are not as marvelous as one might expect. Another disappointment. While the food in Florence was consistently superb, Venetian cuisine was anticlimactic at best. We decided after that first mediocre meal to disregard the recommendations of our hotel, and to rely instead on the recommendations of our friends. This led us to Trattoria alla Madonna, across the Rialto Bridge in the San Polo district.

The Trattoria alla Madonna is on a dark, dank, covered alley just off the Grand Canal. A large lighted sign hanging across the narrow street was our beacon (for we were sure we'd been misdirected) and we arrived just as they opened at seven o'clock. Here waiters bustled about in dinner jackets and long white aprons speaking in four languages. Our waiter, Franco, was efficacious and charming, and the food superb. The white table cloths, the ice covered display of fresh fish, the heavy restaurant silver, the rituals that went with old world service (like presenting the customer with the fish before cooking it) all added up to what I wanted Venice to be like: rare, intimate and lovely.

We found during our stay that the further we got from the Piazza San Marco, the happier we were with Venice. This is when we saw the laundry hanging over the canal, the lush green gardens behind closed gates, cats sunning themselves on a bridge, a view of the sun drenched lagoon at a canal's end.

"This is more like it," I said as we joined the late afternoon strollers on our third day in Venice. We'd spent the day on the island of Murano and had decided to walk back to the hotel from the first quay rather than take the *vaporetto* all the way around Venice to the Grand Canal.

"More like what?" asked Phil dodging a baby carriage being carried by both parents over the footbridge we were crossing.

"More like what I wanted Venice to be like," I said.

"More like a movie," said Phil.

"Well, yes."

"That movie must be forty years old."

"So am I," I pointed out.

"Which is way it's such a great movie!"

Good save.

"Uh huh..."

On our last night in Venice we walked over to the Piazza San Marco after dinner. A small crowd of tourists moved from cafe to cafe listening to the different orchestras. One cafe's orchestra played popular tunes of the last twenty years, while another played all together too much Andrew Lloyd Webber. This night we decided to sit at the cafe playing classical music, not because we're such cultured snobs (though we've been called worse) but because it best suited the mood of the evening. We sat with coffee brought by a liveried waiter with a program of the evening's musical selections. Perfect.

Later, sipping our after dinner drinks, we watched elegantly dressed Italians come and go to the music, well coifed women with little dogs on their laps and handsome men in perfectly tailored suits. We let go of each other's hand just long enough to applaud as the orchestra finished playing. I put my cigar down a moment and discretely kissed Phil's ear.

"This is it," I whispered. "This is the Venice I wanted to see."

I closed my eyes and enjoyed the sensation. The cigar, the moon, the music, the warm spring air, and Phil: It all came together in one perfect, sensuous moment.

"Yes, it is" said Phil quietly, taking one last puff on his cigar before putting it out. "But which one of us is Katherine Hepburn?"

A Nice Boy from a Good Family

Having Once Known Abandon

*By the cigars they smoke, and the composers they love,
ye shall know the texture of men's souls.
– John Galsworthy*

The Cauldron, San Francisco, 1981

Tonight I am more than just horny: Tonight I know exactly what I want.

I have a new boyfriend; which is to say, I'm dating (as is the norm in 1981) three or four men at the same time and the new one, Jan, is my favorite: He's an incredible fuck. Not only does he have a big dick, he knows how to use it and has the kind of staying power one rarely finds: Twenty minutes of fucking is nothing to him, twice that the norm, ninety minutes not unheard of. His prowess and expertise leaves me raw and weak in the knees – and very, very happy. Best of all, he is also my first Master. Part of me thinks I ought to be in love with him; another part knows that love would only lead to disappointment. If the sex is that good, a friend asks me, why blow it? Why ruin it with love? I am forced to agree, though I normally think it is more a question of ruining love with sex than the other way around.

Jan, though, is out of town, and the other men I've been concurrently dating are all busy tonight, so I'm left to my own devices. If I can't have quality, I reason, I can at least have quantity. I feel my fuckhole twitching, wanting dick and cum, wanting to be fucked hard and heavy and long. I have decided tonight to get fucked by as many men as I can, to be filled with cock and cum repeatedly. I want to be dripping spunk when the night is over, to stink of seed. I want to go to bed feeling dirty.

Each sex club South of Market has a specialty; each one caters to a particular audience and taste. The Cauldron is heavily leather, has a water sports area, lots of slings, plenty of space for the usual fucking and sucking, as well as eyebolts conveniently located along it's many walls for bondage and flogging. In a word: It's civilized, and I feel at home here.

I walk around in old boots, torn Levis and no shirt. My body is unremarkable in a city of extraordinary men – except that it is so nubile, so unblemished, so visibly aching for abuse and begging for defilement. I've learned to use this perceived innocence, as well as my boyish (if bearded) face, to the best advantage. I affect a guilelessness that appeals to many, a seemingly natural smile to betray my enthusiasm for all the pain and pleasure that's offered to me. Once I was told that I looked like a Cub Scout gone wrong. I took this as a great compliment: In fact, it's how I wanted to be seen – even if I'd never put it in those words before the trick in question (a man over thirty) spoke them while disheveling my short hair with one massive hand, and slapping my butt with the other, before one final kiss and leaving my bed (and life) forever. This succinct description of the Cub Scout gone wrong will follow for me for years to come.

The line is still short when I arrive at the Cauldron. It is just eleven o'clock, the magic hour for bars and sex clubs in San Francisco on a Saturday night. A moment's pause to check my jacket, and in I go.

Almost at once I feel a hand on my ass. I want to know who it is but don't dare look around for fear of losing the moment. I reach behind me and feel his crotch, feel the hard cock already jutting out of undone army fatigues. I know who it is at once, recognize the ribbed singlet, the mustached kiss on my shoulder. I drop my jeans in response. I bend over a nearby table and let him find his way home, find the hole he wants to fill with his manhood, the manhood I want to steal from him. As he enters, I recognize the girth of his cock, the rapidity of the rhythm as he fucks me. He will cum several times tonight, but this is the first load, the biggest one, and all the other men who fuck me tonight will feel the slickness of his semen on their cocks. Because it's his first fuck of the night; he doesn't last very long. He grunts and groans and I squeeze my hole as tight as I can, urging him to reach his climax. He kisses my shoulder when, after a shudder and a growl, he cums inside me. I turn around and we share a kiss, a smile, and thank each other for the momentary pleasure, for the five minutes diversion. Another kiss and we both move on.

Next is a red-bearded Irishman from Chicago dressed in black leather. He roughly fucks my face before bending me over in a corner and fucking my ass without tenderness or ceremony. His boyfriend, a furry Italian also wrapped in black leather, joins in and fucks my face until the Irishman is finished with my ass, then takes his place. I hear them kiss sloppily as they take turns fucking me, hear their murmured endearments above my bowed head. I take their seed, hear them grunt and groan as they spill it inside me, mixing together with the seed of the first man that fucked me. Some part of me wishes I were a part of their intimacy, a partaker of the kiss and not just the hole they're fucking. When the Italian finishes, they embrace; kiss noisily while I stand awkwardly where I am unable to pass them in the corner we've been fucking in, and just as unable to be a part of what they're sharing. Then they notice me. They smile, each giving me a smack on the lips and a swat on the ass.

"Thanks, boy!"

"Yeah, thanks!"

I smile, mumbling something about it being my pleasure, but they head off arm in arm without listening. How I wish I were a part of what they share, that Jan and I were as intimate in public as we are in private, that we loved each other as these men do. I wish for it but shrug off my discontent in anticipation of who will be next.

I move on.

A man I'm passing pulls me to him. Somewhere in his forties, he is in his prime, the epitome of Daddy-ness. He is furry and mustached, flecked with gray, unshaven, and muscular. He puts me in a lip-lock that I submit to without resistance. I follow his every lead like a well rehearsed dancer with his partner: When the kiss breaks I suck his nipples, lick the sweat from his hairy armpits, then return to his mouth for more kisses. He is a brilliant kisser: His kisses feed my desire, weaken my knees, making me all the more malleable in his calloused hands. There is little I won't do for him, I know. He pulls down my jeans (already undone) and spanks my ass, whispers dirt in my ear about Daddy fucking boy butt, then forces me to my knees to suck his dick.

He continues to talk trash as he fucks my throat, pausing only to slap me across the face with his cock. This is the button that turns off my brain and turns on my cock. I no longer care about anything but keeping him there with me, making him mine. I must have his load: I need to have his essence, to take some part of his manhood away with me when we part.

He pulls me to my feet and pushes me down onto a padded platform. My torn jeans are pulled down to my ankles as I lay prone on my stomach. He mounts me and enters in a single brutal thrust that makes me cry out in pleasure, a loud cry that he mistakes for pain.

"Relax, boy," he whispers in my ear, not stopping. "Breathe deep and take Daddy's dick."

"Yes, Sir," I gasp. "Please keep fucking me, Sir. I can take it, Sir."

He saws away inside me, faster and rougher. I feel his sweat dropping off of his hairy body and onto my smooth skin, feel it trickle down my back to the crack of my ass.

"Fuck!" he screams too soon to suit me. "Fucking fuck, boy! FUCK!"

There are screams of pleasure, the agonies of orgasm, as his furry body thrashes on top of me, his legs shaking, his arms trembling.

"Fuck!" he says one final time before rolling off of me.

Before I get up, someone else mounts me. I turn to the Daddy who only winks and smiles at me. He leans over and kisses me as the newcomer fucks me, whispers sweet words that excite me; they sound so dirty, these endearments amid the squalor of sex, piss and cum. Then the stranger finishes and thanks Daddy for the privilege of fucking me.

"Yeah, he's a damn fine fuckhole," Daddy tells the stranger as they shake hands.

I don't turn around to see who the stranger is, afraid of being disappointed. Besides, it's better this way, not knowing, just being an object that Daddy can share. For the first time I wonder what Daddy's name is.

He catches me looking at him, smiles, and kisses me again.

"You okay, boy?"

"Yes, Sir. Thanks. That was great, Sir."

He smacks my ass and pulls up my jeans before helping me to stand.

"See you," he says with a final kiss and a tweak at my nipples.

"So long," I say, still wondering who he is, what his name is, if I'll ever see him again. Not that any of this matters, not really. I'm getting what I want.

I am on the verge of something, almost trembling within, ready to sail over the waterfall and into the abyss. I want to feel how I feel after a night with Jan: Worn out and well used, sated and sore. Where is he, the one that will do this for me?

I wander about, grabbing crotches, caressing nipples, kissing mustached and bearded mouths, licking leather. More men fuck me, slap my ass, call me 'boy,' kiss me hard in an effort to possess me. But I keep waiting for the ride into oblivion.

Then I see him, handsome and shirtless, in undone Levis and boots. He is surrounded by men: They chew his nipples, suck his cock, lick his balls, eat his ass, burrow into his armpits. He has given himself over to the pleasure of being serviced, but does not participate. But then he sees me approach and reaches out to me. We kiss, our lips meeting across empty space, as the others continue to service him. A few minutes later, he shakes them off like pesky flies and leads me by the seat of my Levis into another corner. Putting his arm around my neck as we walk away, he takes possession of me as no one else has done tonight.

In our corner we continue to kiss. He manhandles my ass and fuckhole as we kiss. I grab and pull on his magnificent cock. How much he wants to fuck me, how much I want him to be inside me. But he takes his time. He plays my body like an instrument, making me gasp in pleasure and pain, making me moan low and cry out: Cry out for him to stop, for more of the same mistreatment. Between my nipples and my nuts, between my mouth and fuckhole, I am a quivering mass of nameless emotions and deeper sensations, lost in the haze of his kisses. Seeing me turned to putty, he's satisfied, pushes me to my knees to fuck my face. I choke on his cock, look up into his face in despair. He smiles back down at me, his lips a cruel grin; and my cock gets even harder. My face is dick whipped before I'm pulled to my feet and pushed over a nearby trashcan. He fucks me fast and furious, hard and brutal. Even after all the dick I've had tonight, it still hurts, still startles me out of my stupor. He fucks me for what seems like forever, for countless minutes, then cums with a scream that echoes over the over-amplified music and through the old warehouse that houses the Cauldron. He pushes me away as he disengages himself, almost knocking me over. I slowly stand upright to see the same cruel smile. Past speaking, I drop to my knees and suck his softening dick, move my mouth up to his flat belly and smooth chest to lick the sweat from his body.

"That's it," he murmurs. "That's a good boy."

When I reach his mouth he kisses me again.

"Didja cum?"

I only now realize that I'd cum without touching myself, not even noticing.

"Yes, Sir."

"Thought so by the way you screamed."

"I screamed?"

"Fuck yeah!"

He kisses me again.

"Thanks. See ya."

"Yeah. So long, Sir."

I walk away before he does, find my way to the coat check and then the door. When I reach 10th Street I realize that the sky is gray. Dawn is almost upon me. Like a vampire or a troll, I rush home to find my bed before light can turn me into dust or stone. I am euphoric, weak-kneed, and exhausted. But now I know the word for what I feel with Jan, for what I wanted to feel all night: No, not love: Abandon.

An AIDS Fundraiser, San Francisco, 1992

I don't know what possessed me to try and explain the Cauldron to the twenty-something queer boys I meet at this rather silly cocktail party being held at the Natural History Museum on a Tuesday night. I tell them about the nights I came crawling home at dawn, euphoric, spent and content. It's as futile as trying to share those golden moments of disco mania: Words can't communicate the importance of these seemingly trivial and narcissistic moments of our collective pasts.

The boys only shake their heads in wonder at their antecedents' depravity. Hearing me tell tales of the Cauldron, the Jaguar, the 1808, the baths and the Catacombs, they look at me aghast and ask:

"But why would you *want* to do that?"

I shrug my shoulders, feeling sorry for them for not knowing the answer already (for if they don't know it now, they never will) but also afraid to tell them. Nor can I explain that now, after losing most of my friends – now, whenever I look at my dying Daddy – I miss those moments more than ever. I just shake my head and shrug.

"It seemed like a good idea at the time."

I can't tell them, these boys who have only known sex with condoms, how I long for rubber-less sex, for the feeling of a cum-filled hole. I tell myself the lie that safe sex is great, that I don't miss the old days; I believe that I have to lie in order to survive the miasma that whirls about me.

I lie and sometimes even believe myself. But having once known abandon, one doesn't want to live with it.

Cigar Party at the Sling, San Francisco, 2001

The club is on Natoma Street, almost directly across from what was once the Cauldron. I feel a rush of nostalgia as we push the door open and go

A Nice Boy from a Good Family

in, following the smell of cigar smoke. I know most of the men there, and they know me. We are fellow survivors, our lives extended years beyond anything we might have once anticipated. Refusing to die, we refuse to stop fucking either. We have all come to an understanding by now: The old days for us are not yet over. We are all long-term survivors and no longer fear condom-less sex, at least not with each other. We have returned to it.

I cut a cigar for my (new) Sir and light it for him before I undress and light one for myself. We are both in our element here. I am collared but allowed to wander off on my own for the evening, getting as much action as I can muster. Smiles are exchanged with new and old friends as I wander from room to room, watching those already playing, looking for those wanting to play.

I don't know the first man who touches my bare ass, fingering the hole, but he is tall and handsome enough, smooth and hard muscled, his cock fat enough to impress me. There is the preliminary kissing and foundling, the cock sucking and the rimming, before he bends me over and prepares to enter me.

"Bareback okay?" he asks in a hoarse whisper, his throat tight with his need to cum.

"I'm poz," I answer. "It's up to you."

He answers by pushing his way in, my hole prepared for sex before we left the house: Clean, greased and ready. He pushes his way in and lets out a small cry of pleasure. Twenty years of being fucked, countless hours of exercising those very specific muscles, and I am pleased that I can still elicit this cry from a stranger, that I'm still a good fuck. My head snaps back in response to the girth of his cock inside me, the bulbous head hitting my prostate.

"Yeah!" is all I say before he pulls out and shoves his way back inside me. And again, "Yeah!"

First fucks never last long. He fucks hard and furious, cumming inside me in a few minutes. He's panting and sweating when it's over, and I'm pleased. As always, I turn around for a kiss, then lick the sweat from his brow. We thank each other as we relight our cigars, exchange names. He's visiting from Amsterdam, which doesn't surprise me since his cock is so superbly Dutch: Fat and beautiful. Another kiss and we both move on.

I watch an extraordinarily well-hung Latin getting an inadequate blowjob. He wants the sucker's throat but isn't getting it. I smile to myself knowing I could do no better with such a huge dick. Then I watch a handsome, bearded man I know slightly, cigar clenched between his teeth, fucking face.

His tattoos dance across his arms as he holds the back of the man's head. I do my best to remember each pixel of this image, knowing that I'll want to recall it perfectly next time I can't get to sleep and reach for my dick and the sedation of a quick wank. My eyes move on to a man in leather, also smoking a cigar, grinding the heel of his boot into a slave's neck, spitting on him, muttering abuse. My cock gets even harder.

I move on.

When I go into the next room, the Latin is suddenly behind me, feeling my butt. I turn and smile.

"How do you like to fuck?" he asks. "Raw?"

"Oh, yeah."

I lie on my back on a padded table and rest my ankles on his shoulders. His cock, huge compared to the rest of his slender frame, finds the target on the first try.

"I like it when an asshole already has cum in it," he whispers leaning forward, his lips almost touching my face. "I love thinking about all the jizz that's inside that butt, how mine is going to join it, mixing together with all those other men's sperm..."

We kiss.

He fucks, pauses, and fucks some more. He's trying to hold back. My head rocks back and forth. I have no words for the pleasure I'm feeling, for the thrill that's running from deep inside and through the rest of me.

"This is how men are supposed to fuck!" he grunts as he thrusts into me. "This is how it's supposed to be! Raw!"

Then he shudders, gasps for breath, and I feel his cock flex and pulse as he shoots his load inside me. He stays in me as long as he can, kisses me with his cock still inside me, rocking in and out until he finally goes soft and exits me with a wet plop that makes us both laugh.

No sooner is he gone, than the bearded man I saw fucking face a few minutes before takes his place. Still chomping on his cigar, he smiles and nods at me as he lines up his less impressive, but certainly more than adequate, dick with my hole. We've fucked before and need no negotiation. I start squeezing before he even enters me; I want to make him feel good, to make him want to cum inside me. Apparently dissatisfied with the head he was getting earlier, he moves quickly towards orgasm, shaking the sweat from his body in the heat of the smoke-filled room, shaking it across my chest and face as he thrashes his groin against me, as he pounds the secret spot that makes me shiver. After he cums, he pulls out and with another nod, smiles his thanks. But I get no kiss, which disappoints me.

I get up, relight my cigar a second time and look for Sir. I find him slapping some pretty boy across the face before spitting into his open mouth and forcing him to his knees. Well, good, he doesn't need me then.

I go back, wandering about for a while before I see the man in leather leaning against a wall, waiting. I approach him, sink to my knees and suck his dick without waiting for permission. His PA knocks against my teeth, though, so I stand up and offer him my butt. He pushes my head down towards the floor, grabs my hips, and fucks me. I feel the cool hardness of the metal inside me; feel the line of posts piercing the underside of his cock. It feels so strange and so good, so dirty and so right. He fucks me for a long time, pounding me, slapping my ass, muttering abuse I can't really hear over the din of the music. He fucks and fucks me, finally cumming with a slow rising scream, a primal call to the gods of desire. He slaps my ass one more time and pulls out.

"Thank you, Sir."

"Sure, boy."

He walks away thinking he's the victor: But I have him inside me. His essence, his manhood is buried deep inside my body. I have his strength and his seed. I know that I'm the conqueror.

My new Latin friend returns to my side, his huge cock arching to heaven. He smiles and leads me to a sling. I get in it with less grace than I'd like to admit to, slipping my booted feet through the loops. His white teeth sparkle as he smiles, even in this dark, blue-smoked room. He is inside me again, his eyes closed, blissful. He moves slowly at first, slowly and steadily, asking me how much I like his dick, how much I like getting fucked, asking how many loads I have up my ass already. I only grunt and groan my responses, unable to make words anymore. With what little mental focus I have, I remember to squeeze and relax, to grab onto to his cock with my hole and let go. His head is nodding back and forth, his eyes closed, as he gets closer. This time he shouts, cries to his Saints in Spanish, as he shoots inside me. Then he opens his eyes again, looks at me and smiles his big broad smile.

Do I want to cum? I demur, knowing I need to wait a little while yet. I am now, as I have always, been the kind of guy that only cums once a night: One huge, multiple orgasm that empties my balls in a series of bone-rattling shots.

My new friend helps me out of the sling, holds and kisses me, his dark slender frame enclosing my stocky, Nordic body. He kisses beautifully and I know without asking that there is a boyfriend somewhere. Men like us, who can give themselves so freely to sex, and with such enthusiasm, always have partners.

I feel myself leak, feel the jizz dribbling down my leg. I want to keep it inside me for as long as I can, though, and head towards the front room where I can sit down with my feet up, maybe even finish that damn cigar. Before I get there, I run into a handsome man I've seen around before, a man so handsome I've always thought him out of my league. The bottoms I see him with are porn star quality and I've kept my admiration to myself, watching him with quiet envy. He's in a leather cop uniform, complete with nightstick and handcuffs. As always, his good looks and haberdashery take my breath away. Wordlessly, he grabs my arm and leads me to another room, bends me over a bench, and cuffs my hands together behind my back. He threatens my butt hole with his nightstick, hitting me across the ass with it just hard enough to make me jump. Then he pushes his cock (not huge but substantial enough to be called big) inside me. He is rough and cruel while he fucks me, looking to hurt rather than please me. This turns me on even more. One gloved hand grabs my jockstrap while the other one slaps my ass. I don't know how many times he's cum already that night, but I sense that this is not the first. This fuck takes a while, a long wicked while that makes me yelp and cry out in pleasure and pain:

"Yes, Sir! Yes, Sir!"

The he smacks my ass hard one more time and cums, shaking and sweating. When he pulls out of me, I get down on my knees to lick his boots in gratitude, a gesture he appreciates. A few minutes later, he pulls me up roughly by the collar locked around my neck and undoes the handcuffs.

"Thank you, Sir!"

"Sure, boy," he says giving me my kiss. "Nothing like an eager bottom."

"Thank you, Sir!"

I give up on my cigar and once again head back towards the front room. It's getting late and I'm sure Sir will want to go home soon. But then, there he is, my favorite fuck buddy in the world: Six-four and bearded, his green eyes flashing, covered with tattoos, and with what is probably the biggest dick I've ever seen outside of a porn video. He takes his cigar out of his mouth and kisses me, both hands on my ass. I feel almost small with him, almost like a boy again. He leads me to a sling and puts me in it. My feet slip into their loops again, and I feel the 0-gage PA pressing at my hole almost at once. It fucking hurts going in but I hold my breath. I know from experience that once it passes the first sphincter, I'll feel only pleasure. I exhale, relax and am there: Euphoria.

I look up at him, at his handsome bearded face, cigar clenched between his teeth, and watch him look down at me, shaking his head and smiling. He keeps pressing into me, pushing his way deeper inside me, reaching places no one has ever touched but him. I babble nonsense, waiting for him to touch bottom, for his pubes to scratch my crotch, for his big hairy balls to slap against my ass. He slowly inches his way down, and I almost cum without touching myself when he does.

I look up and see him smiling again. He begins in earnest now, pushing and pounding, fucking and feeling his way inside me. I forget to squeeze for a few minutes, but he hardly seems to notice. I feel the cold hardness of his PA, feel the girth of his massive manhood. I stroke myself a few times and cum without trying. I shoot ribbons of jizz through the air, feel it splatter all over me, shot after shot flying over my shoulder. My buddy in his excitement can hardly control himself. Seeing me shoot like that sends him over the edge and he hammers inside me like no one has hammered all night, hammers and howls his cry of triumph. The plum-sized head expands and contracts; the shaft pulses: I feel it all as I have felt nothing else that night. I am overcome. Every part of me shivers. I am without words, without thought. I am still somewhere in that abyss called Desire.

Once again I know how it feels: Abandon.

An hour later, on the motorcycle ride home, I cling to Sir more than usual, needing the solid comfort of his sturdy frame and steady mind. I feel the jizz oozing out of me, darkening the seat of my Levis. When we reach home, when I get off the bike, there is a wet spot on the seat. Unbidden, I lick it clean.

Saying *Kaddish*

Dead is dead not done.
– Gertrude Stein

Faith is the most personal (and subjective) of experiences, and something I find difficult to discuss. I am far more likely to write about my sex life than my emotional life – even when the two overlap. To write about my spiritual life is to reveal a part of me I keep far more private than I do my erotic exploits. Public displays of religiosity embarrass me. To watch two lovers kiss on the street fills me with joy; to hear someone cry out the tenants of his or her faith on the street offends, even embarrasses, me.

I suspect others of my ilk share these prejudices: Raised Unitarian, New England bred. Theological discussions in our home, of which there were many, were filled with phrases like, "If there is a god..." We questioned dogmas, rejected absolutes, and sneered at anyone whose beliefs sprang from a fear of death. Nascent Puritans, despite being Unitarian, our parents, like most New Englanders, are suspicious of emotionalism – a prejudice we all inherited. To feel or believe something deeply is no reason to rant and rave as if one were (my parents' most contemptuous epithet) "a damn Southern Baptist!"

My relationship to G-d, then, is the most intimate one I have and not something I'm wont to discuss. Let me instead talk about *being* (though I think one is always *becoming*) a Jew, about being a part of that very precious commodity we call community, and something of my spiritual life will become clear.

Until my first husband David Lourea died, I had been unaware that the assumption among many was that I had converted for him.

"Are you still Jewish?" more than one friend has asked – even recently, almost 12 years since he died.

At first I was startled by the question, even offended. Now I only nod:

"Yes, I am."

Indeed, I think to myself, if I had not been Jewish, had not continued to be a Jew, how would I have made it through these last ten years and not gone mad? Or even lived?

Having grown up Unitarian, becoming a Jew had not been quite so dramatic a step as it might have been for someone raised Catholic or Baptist. I stayed well within the realm of liberal religion, replacing the vagueness of my spiritual roots with something more defined. I grew up in a tradition that, in its avoidance of dogma, embraced questions rather than answers, an existential awareness rather than the discovery of meaning. I was, in short, raised in a faith based on doubt. Even if I was willing, perhaps even wanting, to believe in Something, I continually found myself falling short of faith with my many questions.

As a Jew I keep asking questions, but now have some expectation that there might be answers. More than that, there are traditions, useful tools I can fall back on, the means to continue living when life feels (as it sometimes does) unlivable.

When David was dying he asked that I sit *shiva* for him, to which I readily complied, thinking that I would do what he asked to honor his memory. It was not until he died and I was suddenly surrounded by a community set on taking care of me that I realized why he had extracted the promise from me. He knew I would need not only the comfort offered by community, but looking after as well.

"But what will I do if you die?" I asked him in tears one desperate night when neither of us could sleep.

"Sit *shiva*, say *kaddish*, and look after the animals."

A sad comfort this, but it worked.

The truth is, of course, that death doesn't make sense. Whatever tales we tell, what ever reasons we come up with to accept our pain graciously, whatever lies we tell about G-d's will being acceptable to us: Death, so concrete and so elusive, remains absolutely meaningless. Which is, I think, why *shiva* and ritualized mourning are so important. For seven days the widow has the comfort of cursing G-d if she so desires, a father can blaspheme out of rage each moment he recalls the enormity of his loss. G-d, it's assumed, understands. G-d is none the worse for either our agony or our anger. And in the end, it is in G-d that we find our absolute and final comfort: Our only real comfort being Love.

The last time I saw a death commemorated at a Unitarian church, a candle was snuffed out to symbolize the community's loss. When David died I lit a candle that would last seven days and nights; now I prayed for the coming of G-d's dominion. I wept unashamedly, as I had never wept before. Had my New England ancestors seen me weep they'd have turned their heads away, embarrassed: And I would have done the same in their place.

Shiva is a luxury like nothing I had ever experienced before: The freedom to wail, to ignore people, to leave a room without excusing myself. My only obligations were to hollow David's memory and eat the meals that were prepared for me. Now even eating, always a joke among Jews, became a sacred act.

One never remembers pain accurately, anymore than one remembers euphoria. The mind, clouded with the chemistry of misery or elation, has only a vague recollection of what was felt. What I remember most clearly from David's funeral, of all the images that force themselves in a jumble on my memory, is glancing down at the sleeve of my jacket and seeing that it was oddly discolored in blots and patches. It took another second for me to realize that it was wet with my tears. Crying being a constant for the last few days, I was oblivious to my tears, but in that moment I was suddenly acutely aware both of them and of my pain.

Kaddish seems an odd prayer for a funeral. There is no reference to death, no request for comfort, no refrain that tells us: This life is over: This life will go on. Instead one praises G-d, prays for the coming the Messianic Era, and says: Amen. But repeating it is comforting, especially when surrounded by community. It becomes a meditation, a time to find the spark that dares to hope despite the apparent absurdity and cruelty of death. It had been years since I'd been able to say *kaddish* without crying, even before David's death, the loss of so many friends impacting in so short a time on the compound fracture that was heart. Through *sloshim*, though, through those thirty days of mourning, the tears stopped coming when I prayed. A kind of peace descended; not acceptance exactly (for I am stubborn on this point and take every opportunity to bring the injustice of the early deaths of so many of my friends to G-d's attention), but a lessening of my anger and desperation. Life continues; which is why we mourn for thirty days and get on with it. When I walked the dogs though Golden Gate Park on one the last days of *sloshim*, I noticed that for the first time since David's death, they initiated play during our stroll. Mourning for them was over, too. Yes, life goes one. On that, at least, G-d and I agreed.

We were called the *Davidim*, and his death left not only the expected emptiness, that great hollow in the heart that had loved him for eight years, but with an acute sense of my new status as a single man. Not only was I alone, now I was just *David* – singular. Few things are as sad as being alone after being coupled.

David died in November, and our anniversary, having always been observed with a massive Hanukkah party, loomed before me. The first holiday season alone found me overwhelmed with a mass of invitations when I had little, if any, inclination to celebrate anything. A year later, the second holiday season found me fishing for invitations, reminding people that I was still there and wanting to reunite with the world after being a recluse for the most part of a year. This reemergence led to some sad attempts at dating, dates with men who, while well meaning, were never as smart or funny or handsome as my David had been. I found myself looking for excuses to not see these men again, avoided answering the phone, and found myself feeling more alone than before.

"Who will take care of me?" I asked David in tears, feeling ashamed of myself for being so selfish as I saw him slipping from my life in daily decrements. "Who will look after me when I get sick?"

"I don't know," David said. "I don't know and I worry about it all the time."

He needn't have worried. The same community that looked after me when David died looked after me through a prolonged illness that no one expected me to survive. Being immune compromised, my symptoms were elusive, the defining ones for what I had (what is commonly called cat scratch fever) were absent, and I lost a full third of my body weight, been away from work for three months and in the hospital for a full month, before a bone marrow biopsy discovered the guilty bacteria.

My community had prayed for me, I later learned. I was given *Gates of Healing*, and I prayed for myself, focusing what little mental energy I had left on reading those few lines in the hope of healing. My recovery was not a miracle, not in the true sense. Rather it was a series of events, the right people saying the right thing to the right medical staff, that finally led to the bone marrow biopsy and treatment. Rather than a miracle, I call it *beshert*.

For the next few months, whenever asked how I was doing, my answer was always the same: "I didn't die!" One hears tales of gratitude from those who have escaped death, but until one has experienced it, one can never understand it, not truly. To find pleasure in every breath, to enjoy something as simple as a peanut butter and jelly sandwich, to rediscover my ability to have sex, to just have regular bowel movements (for which there is *brucha*) were all joys for which I could find no words other than, "*Baruch ata Adonai...*"

But I had lost so much weight I was unrecognizable, as well as incredibly weak. My beautiful *tuchas* and thick muscular legs (always points of pride) were gone. Always *zaftig*, I now had sunken cheeks and a waist so thin that my Levis (once worn an inch larger than my waist to accommodate the muscularity of my butt and legs and then worn, sexily I thought, with no belt) slid down my hips to my scrawny thighs. I had aged years in a few months. How wonderful, though, to sit in the examining room and hear my doctor tell me: "You're job is to eat, eat and eat!" What a joy to eat five or six meals a day and still be hungry for ice cream at bedtime. How strange to find friends forcing food on me, bringing me treats, making me meals, finding especially tasty cheeses for me (so full of fat!) to refill the hollows of my cheeks. What could I say each morning but, "*Baruch ata Adonai...*"

Always vain, I found my way back to the gym to rebuild what was lost. My strength returned. My *tuchas* and legs, while never regaining the fullness they'd once had, are no longer an embarrassment to my (considerable) vanity. My cheeks are full and I have my tummy again. Once more, I am back to my muscular *zaftig* self, the body I was always happy to have and share with others. More importantly, 10 years later, I'm alive.

David had hoped, perhaps even prayed, that I would be spared an early death. Fortunate beyond all right, because I was already in a research protocol at the National Institutes of Health (a program I became alerted to by a member of my *havurah*) I had access to protease inhibitors a full year before they were approved for general distribution. My ravaged immune system repaired itself. Months passed into years that no one, least of all me, thought I would ever have.

But even those grateful for their rebirth get the Empty Bed Blues.

To think of how desperate I sometimes felt for want of love when I was young and still unable to understand the difference between intimacy and sex, between love and passion, between need and desire. Only when I found

David and fell in love with him, did these subtleties become clear to me. Far different are the needs of an adult who knows adult pain and adult love, who understands that passion wanes and there must be something there when it fades to hold a couple together, who already understands that two people can never truly be one, just together and be happy in that togetherness.

Not only is G-d great: G-d is Love.

I'd known Phil, although not well, for years before we'd started dating. Only one mutual friend thought of putting us together, an idea I resisted. It was only when I sat listening to the two of them talk one evening that I realized how appropriate a choice he might be for me. Having come close to death, I no longer felt that I had the luxury of waiting for anything, I asked him point blank, "Do you want to date?"

His answer was a surprisingly shy smile before saying, "Sure."

I always had a knee-jerk reaction to gay marriage. At best it was aping heterosexist convention; at worst it was counter-revolutionary. David and I never even wore rings. Our relationship was sanctified in bed, and that was enough for us.

Phil felt differently. He felt our love was worthy of G-d's blessing and our community's support. This was hard to argue with, the points being too strong for archaic (1970s) radical thought, and I agreed to stand beneath a *huppa* with him. Phil was raised Baptist but, having spent more time worshipping with our *havurah* in the past six months than he had in church in the previous five years, agreed to Jewish ritual for our wedding without missing a heartbeat.

Tears, like prayers, come at seemingly dissimilar moments. Just as I was oblivious to the extent of my tears at David's funeral, I was not fully aware of how much I was crying at the wedding until the rabbi handed me a tissue. Just as the funeral is a jumble of desperate images, so is the wedding a series of happy fragments. Neither event is clearly remembered. What is remembered is a happy life together with years stretching before as well as behind us. How odd now to plan for a future, to worry about retirement. How natural to wake up in the morning, and to fall asleep, saying: *Baruch ata Adonai...*

Were I not a Jew, had I not clung to the faith that adopted me as much as I adopted it, I doubt that I'd ever have understood that to experience love is to experience G-d. Thus, when a loved one dies, only G-d can comfort. To love another human being is to seek and find G-d in that person.

Kaddish or *kiddushin*, I learned, all prayers are the same.

Damn the Defining

*It is as useless to fight against the interpretations
of ignorance as to whip the fog.*
– George Eliot

Let us consider:
I'm eleven years and my best friend, Leigh, has come over wearing the brown leather bomber jacket his Dad wore during the Korean War. Leigh and I are already aficionados (if one can be such a thing) of movies featuring young men in black leather jackets. When we saw **Wild Angels** we were enthralled with the genre, exited in ways that we had no words for yet. I've seen **Rebel Without a Cause** repeatedly with the same excitement (despite my disappointment that James Dean never actually wore a black leather jacket in the movie). In a of couple years I'll have an enormous poster of Marlon Brando in **The Wild One** on my wall and masturbate while looking at the image. But today Leigh came over, showing off the jacket that all our friends envy (a small gang of boys pretending to be a motorcycle gang, zooming around our suburban housing track on bicycles with butterfly handlebars), because I want to try on the jacket.

It's even bigger on me than on Leigh (who is a year older) but I'm frightened by what I see when I look in the mirror: Me wearing leather for the first time. I experience the shock of recognition; I know that this is about sex, about something very dirty that I need to keep to myself. A responsible adult has already informed me of the basic mechanics of sex, but I am unprepared for this narcissism, this first fulfillment of a primary fetish. In a year I'll be jerking-off wearing leather gloves, but I don't know that yet. I only know that it frightens me to see my wish fulfilled, so I take the jacket off and hand it back to Leigh. To return to the familiar I start talking about the most recent issue of **Batman**, **Hawkman** or **Justice League of America**; that is, I return to the acceptable realm of the nascent fetishist, comic books.

There are three main categories of guys in the leather bars, and each variety gets what it need and wants from leather sex. First, there are the guys who think that leather is hot and like to cruise and fuck in it. The second group is the men who are into the scene, and who explore their sexuality and their psyches through shared pain and erotic ritual. The third sort is the man for whom leather is something he lives and breathes each waking moment. My friends and I are, for the most part, the ones in the middle. What we share is an exigency to our sexual expression, the need to delve deep inside ourselves to make the normal exchange of power implicit in all sexual encounters explicit. To put it very simply, just to bring a partner to orgasm is a very powerful thing to do; to climax, to know true abandon at that moment, is to give up complete control to one's partner for those few (but interminable) seconds. Through SM the exhilaration of sex is recreated and prolonged through the intensified sensory input we call pain. Endorphins rush the brain giving the recipient a euphoria that surpasses any artificial opiate. All the power (in theory anyway) is in the hands of the giver, power to be savored, enjoyed and cherished. Despite all appearances, despite the sexual fantasies one reads about, there is more love there than most outsiders can imagine.

We share a similar nature, which feels like a primal need, but does it define us? We are each of us the sum of our life's experiences, but does that define us? Or do we dare let others to define us by how we fuck?

Eighteen years later I'm reading a leather-themed issue of **The Advocate***, and it's clear to me that for each man who writes or is interviewed, there is a different interpretation of what leather and leather sex are. One man is so vehement in his insistence that SM is not about conquering death through pain, that I wonder at it. I've been wearing leather for years by this time, enjoying sex with and without SM, am in my first long-term relationship (one wherein I am the boy), and have been published several times in* **Drummer***. I know (for I've read Becker's* **The Denial of Death***) that SM has become, as much as anything else, my defiance of death (and AIDS) through pain. For* within the complex set of circumstances and emotions that are part of every sadomasochistic experience – the need to take or give up control, the power of orgasm, the emotional and physical sense of elation that comes from getting to the other side of pain – there are deeper psychodramas waiting to be acted out, monsters waiting to be dragged from the darkness of the id and into the light where they are confronted and conquered. Whether these psychodramas are the cause or the product of SM is neither here nor there, but the most primal drama is the confronting of one's own mortality.

I was already an active member of the SM scene for a couple of years when AIDS began devastating our community, and I was keenly aware of the ancient link between Thanos and Eros *(Death and Desire)* and (inspired by Jim Wigler's brilliant photography) had begun exploring this theme in my first published erotica. Now pain became the symbol for the plague in my psyche. If I could take, even overcome, intense physical pain, I would survive the emotional pain I was certain to endure. More importantly, every lash of the whip brought me closer to understanding the most primal of fears, that of my own demise. Thanos *was the monster I defied (as most people do, whether they know it or not) through* Eros – *only pain was a part of* Eros *and in the most subterranean workings of my psyche I defied Death by flirting with it through an agony that became my ecstasy. How the man interviewed in* **The Advocate** *couldn't see this, I would never understand.*

What I do understand, though, is that this need for unorthodox sexual expression is, as much as being queer, ingrained at an early age. I was not the only one, clearly, who let himself get caught when playing cops and robbers so he would be tied up, nor the only one to pretend he was being kidnapped, blindfolded and restrained. Sex with men was only added to this mix of confusing, contradictory impulses when masturbation was joined to my fantasies. I am not, and never was alone.

There are those perverts who think the rest of the world is denying itself the interior dramas that we act out for that rare but acute combination of sexual and emotional release. I've never thought this was the case. I suspect, though, that, for better or worse, we live closer to the subconscious than the rest of world, and with this closeness comes the need to express what others might only understand intellectually. When most people discover something in themselves that makes them uncomfortable – an unexpected sexual arousal, an erotic dream that disturbs them for all it implies – they might talk about it with a friend or therapist, but more than likely they suppress it, ignore it, and hope it will go away. Perverts, on the other hand, will not only talk about the erotic disruption with anyone who will listen, but find someway to act out the dream, to explore the unexpected arousal, just to see where it leads them. This may not explain our sexuality, of course, but it does, perhaps, inform it.

As much as I love wearing leather (and rubber, and uniforms, and the rest of it), I've never felt comfortable calling myself a Leather Man. It's as if that single definition might limit me, make me less who I am by confining me within the label.

I am walking to the gym on a fine Indian summer afternoon, wearing shorts, a polo shirt, and white tennis shoes, when I run into my friend Roger Klorese walking in the opposite direction. Roger introduces me to a friend of his who, on learning that he has read my stories in **Drummer***, looks me over and, obviously disappointed, says, "You're not what I expected." I want to ask him what the hell he did expect. Should I be in full leather on a warm sunny day while walking to the gym to suit his imagined version of me? Was I not serious enough, not appropriately menacing when we were introduced? Roger saves the moment by saying, "David never is what people expect."*

We part and I think of an old cartoon in **Drummer** *wherein a man in full leather is sitting at a bar and moaning to the barkeep, "You know why I don't have a better job? Because I won't wear a fucking uniform!" My point exactly. I don't wear it everyday, nor do I want to. Leather is the vestment I don for the appropriate ritual, not what I wear for the workaday world. Or as some like to put it: It's eveningwear. As comfortable as I am in leather, to wear it everyday would diminish its force for me, make it less powerful, and I want it retain its hold on my brain, on my cock and balls. A man I was cruising online was disappointed because I don't wear black leather boots everyday to work. Apparently a serious leather man would. Even one who works as an executive for a Fortune 500 company? I wanted to ask, but didn't.*

Yet I take great pleasure in wearing my collar to the gym, locked around my neck and in plain view for all to see while I work out and shower. I want the world to know that someone calls me his boy, that I'm proud of belonging to him, and that I'm not another desperate unattached boy loose in the City, looking for a Daddy. That part of me, the boy, is day to day. That is the core part of my leather persona that never changes, the one that is shared at large through the simple gesture of wearing my collar to the gym. Part of my pleasure in wearing it is my feeling of solidarity with the other boys wearing their collars, men with whom I don't speak but share a nod; and part of it is that it disturbs some of the less sophisticated men in the locker room, though they are usually out-of-towners; for this is San Francisco, of course, and hardly anyone looks twice.

As the late, great dominatrix Cynthia Slater once told me when I confessed my trepidation about attending one of her famous mixed SM parties at the Catacombs for the first time, "You don't have to prove anything to anyone. The only one you have to impress is yourself." With that valuable lesson, I navigated my way through San Francisco's leather world and found a home.

Coming out into leather just when the perceived rigidity of what is now romantically referred to as the Old Guard was waning, I still felt that there were expectations – from both within and without the Leather Community – regarding dress and behavior: Expectations that had to be either met or dismissed. In my twenties I liked to wear a black hankie in the hip pocket of my jeans while wearing a polo shirt and deck shoes, just to make a point about what other people's initial perceptions of me might be: Most assumed (I had no doubt) that I was too nice a boy to do such nasty things; others thought (I was certain) that a serious pervert would dress differently. As it turned out, though, no one gave a damn. People on the street still spoke to me as before, and (more importantly at the time) men on motorcycles continued offering to take me for a ride. In short, there was no rejection from the people I met casually at dinner parties or from the men in full leather I wanted to play with so desperately. I soon forgot what or whom I was defying. What was the point of being an iconoclast if all I really wanted to be was myself? Cynthia Slater's words rang truer than ever.

Which is why I stopped labeling myself for the convenience of others, labels being as limiting as they are annoying. If I list those communities that I feel myself a part of – though as diverse and confusing a list as you're likely to see – you might have a hint of who I am. But don't presume to define me as one thing or the other, for I will resist any restrictions that those words might infer. Mutual respect, the cornerstone of the Leather (for want of a better word) Community since its inception, allows me this freedom.

I now offer that same freedom and respect to you.

An Afterward:
Some Notes about this Book, The Reasons for Writing It, and the Inevitable Accusations of Narcissism

Conserve the powers of feeling which should by rights
be directed towards those we love
and which are wasted on those who die.
– Lawrence Durrell

    To write about oneself, let alone to seek to publish that writing, requires a degree of ego that I am uncomfortable admitting to; but the truth is that a healthy ego, a certain amount of self-love, is required if one is to write at all. The self-effacing can not write because they do not believe in themselves or in what they have to say. Similarly, successful romance writers are successful because they believe in what they are writing: a truth that is easily transposed to my own small success as a writer of erotic fiction over the last quarter century: I believe in Eros, in Passion, and in, for want of a better word, Abandon.
    The worst part about writing about oneself, apart from the inevitable, if not unjustified, accusations of narcissism, is one's own confrontation with the truth. To a certain degree, one needs to protect others by changing names, dates or places; but to what degree does one protect oneself? I won't pretend that I have told the whole truth, or even that my perspective isn't, as it

inevitably must be, self-serving at times. Yet I hope that there are no glaring omissions, no reason for any witness to the tales told herein, to curse me for my audacity or bias. Truth is not compulsive disclosure, after all, but the essence of authenticity that a reader will recognize and believe. It is up to the reader to decide as to my success.

The great Chinese curse is: "May you live in interesting times." And my generation of queer men (at least those of us who have survived) has certainly lived in "interesting times." And it has often felt like a curse.

To the ancient Greeks, Eros and Thanos were not gods so much as primal forces, cosmic twins constantly in each other's company. To my generation, this duality was made more explicit in life than in the inevitable nightmares we hoped to forget. Some of us floundered but still found reasons to laugh, love, continue fucking; others stayed home, pulled their blinds and prepared to die the slow death of the dismal. The chances of survival were about the same either way. Of the people I knew and was friendly with in 1982, barely ten percent are alive today, and so I add to my reasons for assembling these disparate pieces into one volume: the need to bear witness to, and to celebrate what once was a wonderful time (roughly 1978 to 1984) in my life; and to remember how swiftly it all came to a close.

To survive is to live, to live is to remember; to remember is to love, and to love is to celebrate life. Despair is the only sin.

Most of the pieces included here were written because I was asked to write them, or at least asked to submit them, for consideration for specific publications. Others were written in response to a Call for Entries.

An **Apparent Proximity** was begun for *Boyfriends from Hell*, but put aside in favor of the **The Lousy, Rotten, No Good, Son-of-a-Bitch, Goddamn Bastard**, a relationship I felt far more hellish if only due to my *naiveté* at that time in my life.

When I saw the call for entries for *Afterwords: Real Sex from Gay Men's Diaries* I was confronted with an embarrassment of riches. I culled my diaries and came up with twice the requested page limit. I submitted the whole manuscript in the hope that (the very kind) Kevin Bentley could edit it down to something manageable. In the end, he eliminated the footnotes (the completion of which took more than a healthy ego to complete) and made a few minor cuts, leaving most of it intact, and the longest piece in that anthology. It was also one of the few actual diaries in the anthology.

Two Weddings, One *Tuchas* was written, and accepted, for an anthology but was later cut by the publisher. I liked what I had written, however, and believed it to be a story worth the telling, and perhaps even representative of those desperate years.

The Seduction of an Innocent began as a series of essays written for an amateur comic book 'zine, and was later condensed for an anthology for which it was rejected. It has been substantially rewritten since then, and I hope much improved.

"And What Shall I Do in Illyria?" was originally written for, and published in, the San Francisco edition of *Frontiers* as an independent piece. Composed at a time when my own life expectancy was short, its tone is somber at the very least. After falling in love and gaining early access to protease inhibitors, I wrote **Life After Life** and then **I Bought the Plot – Now What?** The three pieces form a kind of trilogy tracing life from the nadir of those tragic years to the subsequent years of cautious hope, and finally a re-embracement of life.

For several years running, I wrote pieces for *San Francisco Frontiers'* annual (coinciding with the Folsom Street Fair) Leather Week issue. I include the first, **How I Fell into the Wrong Crowd**, and the last, **Damn the Defining** in this collection.

Many thanks to all of the editors I worked with, all of whom encouraged me at a time I needed encouraging, most notably: Phil Julian, Wickie Stamps, Kevin Bentley, Lawrence Schimel, and the late Robert Davolt whose belief in my voice spurred me forward in both life and love. A special thank you also goes out to the lovely Jenne King who thought of the title for this collection. And finally, many thanks to the man who loves me, my husband and my Sir, and my reason to write. Sweet Daddy, I love you.

About the Author
David May

Starting out in life as a nice boy from a good family looking desperately for the wrong crowd, David May started writing as a child. After graduating from UC Santa Cruz, he moved to San Francisco where he initially gained notoriety in 1984 when his first story, **Cutting Threads**, which was published in *Drummer,* sparking both controversy and praise from readers. A regular contributor to *Drummer* until its demise, May's work has also appeared in *Honcho, Mach, Advocate Men, Unzipped, Inches, Frontiers, Lambda Book Report, Harvard Gay & Lesbian Review, Cat Fancy, International Leatherman* and *Manifest Review.* David May's work, both fiction and nonfiction, can also be found in *Kosher Meat, Best of Gay Erotica 2003, Best of Gay Erotica 2007, Afterwords: Real Sex From Gay Men's Diaries, Bar Stories, Queer View Mirror, Flesh and the Word 3, The Mammoth Book of New Gay Erotica, Bears* and many other anthologies. In 2002 he moved to Seattle where he lives with, and is owned by, his Sir and two cats.

David May is also the author of:

- *Madrugada: A Cycle of Erotic Fictions*
- *Butch Bottom & the Absent Daddy and Ten Other Leather Love Stories*

Find this book and others at your local bookstore, Amazon.com and TheNazcaPlainsCorp.com.

MADRUGADA
A CYCLE OF EROTIC FICTIONS

DAVID MAY

A BONER BOOK

BUTCH BOTTOM
&
THE ABSENT DADDY
and Ten Other Leather Love Stories

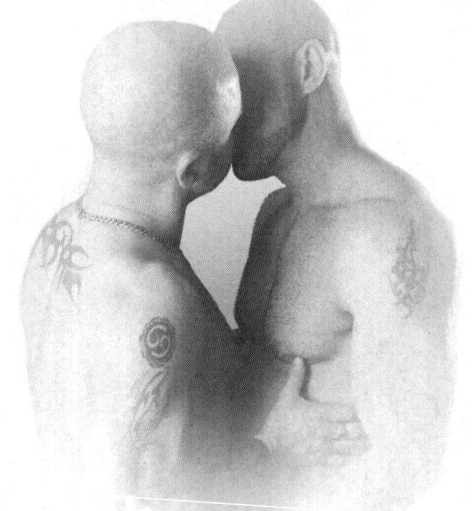

DAVID MAY

A BONER BOOK

Having Once Known Abandon contrasts three nights in 1981, 1992 and 2001: Two nights of abandon between which he confronts the ignorant bliss of young queer men who will never know the kind of sexual freedom and passion he once took for granted.

Two Weddings, One *Tuchas* shares the worst and best of the desperate years – days and nights spent looking for the comfort and release that only a new lover can provide, even as his friends died around him. May negotiates painful memories and a few honest regrets in this story about and the consequences of avoiding the depth of his grief.

First appearing in *Drummer*, **Hole** recalls a birthday gangbang wherein the birthday boy, May himself, is bound and blindfolded and made the sexual plaything of a series of nameless men whose faces he never sees.

Causing a stir of controversy when it first appeared in *Frontiers*, **How I Fell in with the Wrong Crowd** recalls the days and nights spent seeking pleasure and passion before the AIDS epidemic. Criticized by some for its expressed lack of regret, and praised by others for its forthrightness, the piece established May as a commentator on queer life.

Gathered from *Drummer*, *Frontiers* and numerous anthologies, this is the first collection of David May's nonfiction. These pieces form a fragmented autobiography wherein the Erotic and the Spiritual are never at odds, where Love and Lust were frequently confused, where Death is faced with trepidation and fury, and where Life continues to be worth living. Amid the accumulated losses of a life lived at what had once been an oasis of sexual freedom, a city that changed almost overnight into the epicenter of a disaster, May bares witness to one man's survival in "Interesting Times."

A Nice Boy from a Good Family... ***tells all!***

Bringing together the best of David May's nonfiction, *A Nice Boy from a Good Family* recalls episodes from a life lived in "Interesting Times." Beginning with a pre-adolescent obsession with comic books that lead to his eventual sexual awakening, and ending in the spiritual journey necessitated by the AIDS epidemic and his own HIV status, May is unflinching as he narrates the carefree years before AIDS through the subsequent years of desperation and loss. With few regrets, May describes his life as a sexually active and eager young man that embraced sadomasochism in the in the late 1970s, through the loss of his Daddy in 1992, his own brush with death, and the subsequent re-embracement of life and hope with his new Sir in the 1990s.

In **Something Sensational to Read on the Train** May shares the highlights from his diaries from 1978 to 1984, years spent in sexual experimentation during which he negotiated his way through San Francisco's gay sex scene, meeting and bedding some of the well-known men of the time.

An Apparent Proximity is a cautionary tale of a foolish love affair allowed to linger on too long. The story reminds the reader "the red flags are not motioning you forward," something May learns a little too late.

With ***Mein Yiddishe Tate*** May shares the intimate details of a life lived with his first great love, bisexual activist Dr. David Lourea, and the devastating loss that followed.